THE GLENCOE LITERATURE LIBRARY

# The Tragedy of Julius Caesar

## with Related Readings

Glencoe McGraw-Hill

New York, New York   Columbus, Ohio   Woodland Hills, California   Peoria, Illinois

## Acknowledgments

Grateful acknowledgment is given authors, publishers, photographers, museums, and agents for permission to reprint the following copyrighted material. Every effort has been made to determine copyright owners. In case of any omissions, the Publisher will be pleased to make suitable acknowledgments in future editions.

From *Fall of the Roman Republic: Six Lives* by Plutarch, translated by Rex Warner (Penguin Classics, 1958). Copyright © Rex Warner, 1958. Reprinted by permission of Penguin Books Ltd.

"A Eulogy to Dr. Martin Luther King, Jr." by Robert F. Kennedy. Reprinted by permission.

"The Voter" from *Girls at War and Other Stories* by Chinua Achebe, copyright © 1972, 1973 by Chinua Achebe. Used by permission of Doubleday, a division of Random House, Inc.

"Geraldo No Last Name" from *The House on Mango Street*. Copyright © 1984 by Sandra Cisneros. Published by Vintage Books, a division of Random House, Inc. and in hardcover by Alfred A. Knopf in 1994. Reprinted by permission of Susan Bergholz Literary Services, New York. All rights reserved.

"The Legend" by Garrett Hongo. Reprinted by permission of the author.

NOTE: This classic play deals with ambition, politics, betrayal, and murder. Certain words, phrases, references, and situations may offend some readers.

**Cover art:** *Morte di Giulio Cesare*. Camuccini Vincenzo (1773–1844). Museo di Capodimonte, Napoli, Italy/Scala/Art Resource, NY.

*Glencoe/McGraw-Hill*

A Division of The **McGraw·Hill** Companies

Send all inquiries to:
**Glencoe/McGraw-Hill**
8787 Orion Place
Columbus, OH 43240

ISBN 0-07-824889-2
Printed in the United States of America
  2 3 4 5 6 7 8 9 026 05 04 03 02 01

# Contents

## The Tragedy of Julius Caesar

*Continued*

Contents *Continued*

# The Tragedy
# of
# Julius Caesar

**William Shakespeare**

# Cast of Characters

**JULIUS CAESAR:** ambitious military leader and politician; the most powerful man in Rome

**CALPHURNIA:** wife of Caesar

**MARCUS BRUTUS:** friend of Caesar, appointed by him to high office in the Roman government; a believer in the republic and member of the conspiracy against Caesar

**PORTIA:** wife of Brutus and daughter of a Roman patriot

**LUCIUS:** servant of Brutus

**CAIUS CASSIUS:** brother-in-law of Brutus and member of the conspiracy against Caesar

**MARK ANTONY:** friend of Caesar, senator, and eloquent orator; member of the triumvirate, the three-man governing body that ruled Rome after Caesar's death

**OCTAVIUS CAESAR:** Caesar's great-nephew and official heir; member of the triumvirate

**M. AEMILIUS LEPIDUS:** military leader and member of the triumvirate

## Conspirators Against Caesar

| | | |
|---|---|---|
| CASCA | METELLUS CIMBER | TREBONIUS |
| CINNA | DECIUS BRUTUS | CAIUS LIGARIUS |

## Senators

| | | |
|---|---|---|
| CICERO | PUBLIUS | POPILIUS LENA |

## Tribunes (Public officials)

| | |
|---|---|
| FLAVIUS | MURELLUS |

**TITINIUS:** an officer in the army of Cassius

## Officers and Soldiers in the Army of Brutus

| | | |
|---|---|---|
| LUCILIUS | MESSALA | VOLUMNIUS |
| YOUNG CATO | FLAVIUS | |

## Servants of Brutus

| | | |
|---|---|---|
| CLITUS | STRATO | VARRUS |
| CLAUDIO | DARDANIUS | |

## Others

A SOOTHSAYER (one who predicts the future)

ARTEMIDORUS OF CNIDOS: teacher of rhetoric

CINNA: a poet

PINDARUS: servant of Cassius

ANOTHER POET

SERVANTS TO CAESAR, ANTONY, AND OCTAVIUS; CITIZENS, GUARDS, SOLDIERS

3   **mechanical:** of the artisans' economic and social class.
4   **sign:** tools and clothes.

10   **in respect of:** in comparison with.
11   **cobbler:** clumsy worker or mender and maker of shoes. The Cobbler plays on the word's double meaning. Murellus and Flavius fail to understand his pun at first and keep pressing him to reveal a trade he has already identified.
13   **use:** practice.

16   **out:** angry.
16–17   **if you be out:** if your shoes are worn out.

22   **awl** a tool for making holes in leather. The Cobbler puns on the words *all, awl,* and *withal,* which means "nevertheless."

# Act 1

## SCENE 1. Rome. A street.

[*Enter* FLAVIUS, MURELLUS, *and certain* COMMONERS *over the stage.*]

**FLAVIUS.** Hence! Home, you idle creatures, get you home!
Is this a holiday? What, know you not,
Being mechanical,° you ought not walk
Upon a laboring day without the sign°
5      Of your profession? Speak, what trade art thou?

**CARPENTER.** Why, sir, a carpenter.

**MURELLUS.** Where is thy leather apron and thy rule?
What dost thou with thy best apparel on?
You, sir, what trade are you?

10 **COBBLER.** Truly, sir, in respect of° a fine workman, I am but, as
you would say, a cobbler.°

**MURELLUS.** But what trade art thou? Answer me directly.

**COBBLER.** A trade, sir, that, I hope, I may use° with a safe
conscience, which is indeed, sir, a mender of bad soles.

15 **FLAVIUS.** What trade, thou knave? Thou naughty knave,
what trade?

**COBBLER.** Nay, I beseech you, sir, be not out° with me; yet, if
you be out,° sir, I can mend you.

**MURELLUS.** What mean'st thou by that? Mend me, thou saucy
fellow?

20 **COBBLER.** Why, sir, cobble you.

**FLAVIUS.** Thou art a cobbler, art thou?

**COBBLER.** Truly, sir, all that I live by is with the awl;° I meddle
with no tradesman's matters, nor women's matters; but
withal, I am indeed, sir, a surgeon to old shoes; when they

| 26 | **neat's leather:** cowhide. The Cobbler claims that his shoes have been worn by as fine men as ever walked in shoes. |
|---|---|

| 31 | **triumph:** triumphal celebration. (The triumph was held to celebrate Julius Caesar's defeat of two sons of Pompey the Great, his former rival. Caesar gained control over Rome when he defeated Pompey in 48 B.C.) |
|---|---|
| 33 | **tributaries:** captured enemies who pay tribute, or ransom money, for their release. |
| 34 | **captive bonds:** the chains of prisoners. |

| 43 | **but:** only. |
|---|---|

| 45 | **Tiber:** a river running through Rome. |
|---|---|
| 46 | **replication:** echo. |

| 49 | **cull out a holiday:** pick out this day as a holiday. |
|---|---|

| 51 | **Pompey's blood:** Pompey's sons. |
|---|---|

| 54 | **intermit:** hold back. |
|---|---|

| 58–60 | **Draw them to . . . of all:** Flavius wants the commoners to weep into the Tiber until the river's lowest water reaches its highest banks. |
|---|---|
| 61 | **whe'er . . . mov'd:** whether their humble spirits have not been touched. |

25      are in great danger, I recover them. As proper men as ever
         trod upon neat's leather° have gone upon my handiwork.

    **FLAVIUS.**    But wherefore art not in thy shop today?
         Why dost thou lead these men about the streets?

    **COBBLER.**    Truly, sir, to wear out their shoes, to get myself into
30      more work. But indeed, sir, we make holiday to see Caesar
         and to rejoice in his triumph.°

    **MURELLUS.**    Wherefore rejoice? What conquest brings he home?
         What tributaries° follow him to Rome,
         To grace in captive bonds° his chariot wheels?
35      You blocks, you stones, you worse than senseless things!
         O you hard hearts, you cruel men of Rome,
         Knew you not Pompey? Many a time and oft
         Have you climb'd up to walls and battlements,
         To tow'rs and windows, yea, to chimney tops,
40      Your infants in your arms, and there have sate
         The livelong day, with patient expectation,
         To see great Pompey pass the streets of Rome;
         And when you saw his chariot but° appear,
         Have you not made an universal shout,
45      That Tiber° trembled underneath her banks
         To hear the replication° of your sounds
         Made in her concave shores?
         And do you now put on your best attire?
         And do you now cull out a holiday?°
50      And do you now strew flowers in his way,
         That comes in triumph over Pompey's blood?°
         Be gone!
         Run to your houses, fall upon your knees,
         Pray to the gods to intermit° the plague
55      That needs must light on this ingratitude.

    **FLAVIUS.**    Go, go, good countrymen, and, for this fault,
         Assemble all the poor men of your sort;
         Draw them to Tiber banks and weep your tears
         Into the channel, till the lowest stream
60      Do kiss the most exalted shores of all.°

[*Exit all the* COMMONERS.]

         See, whe'er their basest mettle be not mov'd;°
         They vanish tongue-tied in their guiltiness.
         Go you down that way towards the Capitol,

**64–65** **Disrobe the images . . . ceremonies:** Flavius directs Murellus to remove any decorations from the statues.

**67** **feast of Lupercal:** religious festival for a god worshiped by shepherds as a protector of flocks.

**69** **trophies:** decorations honoring Caesar.

**70** **vulgar:** common people.

**72–73** **These growing . . . pitch:** Plucking feathers from a bird's wings prevents it from flying. Flavius uses this metaphor for his plan to keep Caesar's power at an **ordinary pitch,** or medium height.

**6–9** **Forget not . . . curse:** Caesar, who has no children, refers to a traditional belief that barren women could become fertile if they were struck by leather thongs carried by runners who passed through Rome on the feast of Lupercal.

This way will I. Disrobe the images,
65      If you do find them deck'd with ceremonies.°

**MURELLUS.**   May we do so?
You know it is the feast of Lupercal.°

**FLAVIUS.**   It is no matter, let no images
Be hung with Caesar's trophies.° I'll about,
70      And drive away the vulgar° from the streets;
So do you too, where you perceive them thick.
These growing feathers pluck'd from Caesar's wing
Will make him fly an ordinary pitch,°
Who else would soar above the view of men
75      And keep us all in servile fearfulness.

*[They exit.]*


## SCENE 2. Rome. A public place.

*[Enter* CAESAR, ANTONY *for the course,* CALPHURNIA, PORTIA, DECIUS, CICERO, BRUTUS, CASSIUS, CASCA, CITIZENS, *and a* SOOTHSAYER; *after them* MURELLUS *and* FLAVIUS.*]*

**CAESAR.**   Calphurnia!

**CASCA.**                 Peace, ho, Caesar speaks.

*[All fall silent as* CAESAR *calls for his wife.]*

**CAESAR.**                                   Calphurnia!

**CALPHURNIA.**   Here, my lord.

**CAESAR.**   Stand you directly in Antonio's way
When he doth run his course. Antonio!

5     **ANTONY.**   Caesar, my lord?

**CAESAR.**   Forget not in your speed, Antonio,
To touch Calphurnia; for our elders say,
The barren, touched in this holy chase,
Shake off their sterile curse.°

**ANTONY.**                I shall remember;
10     When Caesar says, "Do this," it is perform'd.

**CAESAR.**   Set on, and leave no ceremony out.     *[Flourish.]*

**SOOTHSAYER.**   Caesar!

**CAESAR.**   Ha! Who calls?

15 **press:** crowd.

17 **turn'd to hear:** Caesar turns his good ear to the Soothsayer (he was deaf in one ear).

18 **ides of March:** March 15. In the Roman calendar, a day in the middle of every month was called the ides.

25 **order . . . course:** progress of the race.

28 **gamesome:** fond of games and sports.
29 **quick:** lively.

32 **of late:** lately.

34 **was wont to:** used to.

35–36 **You bear . . . loves you:** Cassius uses the metaphor of a rider holding a tight rein on an unfamiliar horse to suggest Brutus's unfriendly behavior toward him.

37–39 **Be not . . . upon myself:** If I have seemed withdrawn, my displeased looks have been turned only on myself.
40 **passions of some difference:** conflicting emotions.
42 **Which give . . . behaviors:** Which might blemish my conduct.

45 **Nor . . . further:** Nor should you think any more of.

**CASCA.**   Bid every noise be still; peace yet again!

15   **CAESAR.**   Who is it in the press° that calls on me?
　　　I hear a tongue shriller than all the music,
　　　Cry "Caesar!" Speak, Caesar is turn'd to hear.°

**SOOTHSAYER.**   Beware the ides of March.°

**CAESAR.**　　　　　　　　　　　　What man is that?

**BRUTUS.**   A soothsayer bids you beware the ides of March.

20   **CAESAR.**   Set him before me, let me see his face.

**CASSIUS.**   Fellow, come from the throng, look upon Caesar.

**CAESAR.**   What say'st thou to me now? Speak once again.

**SOOTHSAYER.**   Beware the ides of March.

**CAESAR.**   He is a dreamer, let us leave him. Pass.

*[They exit. BRUTUS and CASSIUS remain.]*

25   **CASSIUS.**   Will you go see the order of the course?°

**BRUTUS.**   Not I.

**CASSIUS.**   I pray you do.

**BRUTUS.**   I am not gamesome;° I do lack some part
　　　Of that quick° spirit that is in Antony.
30　　Let me not hinder, Cassius, your desires;
　　　I'll leave you.

**CASSIUS.**   Brutus, I do observe you now of late;°
　　　I have not from your eyes that gentleness
　　　And show of love as I was wont to° have.
35　　You bear too stubborn and too strange a hand
　　　Over your friend that loves you.°

**BRUTUS.**　　　　　　　　　　　　Cassius,
　　　Be not deceiv'd: if I have veil'd my look,
　　　I turn the trouble of my countenance
　　　Merely upon myself.° Vexed I am
40　　Of late with passions of some difference,°
　　　Conceptions only proper to myself,
　　　Which give some soil, perhaps, to my behaviors;°
　　　But let not therefore my good friends be griev'd
　　　(Among which number, Cassius, be you one),
45　　Nor construe any further° my neglect,
　　　Than that poor Brutus, with himself at war,

48    **mistook your passion:** misunderstood your feelings.

49–50  **By means . . . cogitations:** Because of this, I have kept important thoughts to myself.

58    **shadow:** reflection.

58–62  **I have heard . . . eyes:** Cassius claims that many highly respected Roman citizens, groaning under the oppression of Caesar's rule, wished that Brutus would recognize his own worth.

68–70  **I, your . . . not of:** I, your mirror, will reveal without exaggeration what you do not yet know about yourself.

71    **jealous on:** suspicious of.

72–78  **Were I . . . dangerous:** If I were a laughingstock or used to cheaply offering my affection to anyone, or if you know me to slander men after fawning on them, or if you know me to proclaim friendship to the common crowd while drinking, then consider me dangerous.

83    **wherefore:** why.

Forgets the shows of love to other men.

CASSIUS.   Then, Brutus, I have much mistook your passion,°
By means whereof this breast of mine hath buried
50  Thoughts of great value, worthy cogitations.°
Tell me, good Brutus, can you see your face?

BRUTUS.   No, Cassius; for the eye sees not itself
But by reflection, by some other things.

CASSIUS.   'Tis just,
55  And it is very much lamented, Brutus,
That you have no such mirrors as will turn
Your hidden worthiness into your eye,
That you might see your shadow.° I have heard
Where many of the best respect in Rome
60  (Except immortal Caesar), speaking of Brutus
And groaning underneath this age's yoke,
Have wish'd that noble Brutus had his eyes.°

BRUTUS.   Into what dangers would you lead me, Cassius,
That you would have me seek into myself
65  For that which is not in me?

CASSIUS.   Therefore, good Brutus, be prepar'd to hear;
And since you know you cannot see yourself
So well as by reflection, I, your glass
Will modestly discover to yourself
70  That of yourself which you yet know not of.°
And be not jealous on° me, gentle Brutus;
Were I a common laughter, or did use
To stale with ordinary oaths my love
To every new protester; if you know
75  That I do fawn on men and hug them hard,
And after scandal them; or if you know
That I profess myself in banqueting
To all the rout, then hold me dangerous.°

[*Flourish and shout.*]

BRUTUS.   What means this shouting? I do fear the people
80  Choose Caesar for their king.

CASSIUS.                                    Ay, do you fear it?
Then must I think you would not have it so.

BRUTUS.   I would not, Cassius, yet I love him well.
But wherefore° do you hold me here so long?

85–87   **If it be aught . . . indifferently:** If it is anything that concerns the public welfare, I will face honor and death impartially.

88   **speed:** favor.

91   **favor:** appearance.

94–96   **for my single . . . myself:** Personally, I would rather not live than live in awe of another human being.

101   **chafing with her shores:** dashing into the shores (as if angry with them for their restraint).

102   **Dar'st thou:** Do you dare?

105   **Accoutred:** dressed in armor.

108   **lusty sinews:** vigorous muscles.

109   **stemming . . . controversy:** making headway against the river's flow in a spirit of rivalry.

112   **Aeneas:** (i nē′ əs) Legendary Trojan warrior and founder of Rome, who, when the Greeks burned the city of Troy, fled carrying his father, Anchises, on his back.

117   **bend his body:** bow.

122   **His coward lips . . . fly:** Cassius uses the metaphor of soldiers abandoning their color, or flag, to say that Caesar's lips turned pale.

123   **bend:** glance, look.

124   **his:** its.

What is it that you would impart to me?
85       If it be aught toward the general good,
Set honor in one eye and death i' th' other,
And I will look on both indifferently;°
For let the gods so speed° me, as I love
The name of honor more than I fear death.

90   **CASSIUS.** I know that virtue to be in you, Brutus,
As well as I do know your outward favor.°
Well, honor is the subject of my story:
I cannot tell what you and other men
Think of this life; but for my single self,
95       I had as lief not be as live to be
In awe of such a thing as I myself.°
I was born free as Caesar; so were you;
We both have fed as well, and we can both
Endure the winter's cold as well as he;
100      For once, upon a raw and gusty day,
The troubled Tiber chafing with her shores,°
Caesar said to me, "Dar'st thou,° Cassius, now
Leap in with me into this angry flood,
And swim to yonder point?" Upon the word,
105      Accoutred° as I was, I plunged in,
And bade him follow; so indeed he did.
The torrent roar'd, and we did buffet it
With lusty sinews,° throwing it aside
And stemming it with hearts of controversy;°
110      But ere we could arrive the point propos'd,
Caesar cried, "Help me, Cassius, or I sink!"
I, as Aeneas,° our great ancestor,
Did from the flames of Troy upon his shoulder
The old Anchises bear, so from the waves of Tiber
115      Did I the tired Caesar. And this man
Is now become a god, and Cassius is
A wretched creature, and must bend his body°
If Caesar carelessly but nod on him.
He had a fever when he was in Spain,
120      And when the fit was on him, I did mark
How he did shake—'tis true, this god did shake;
His coward lips did from their color fly,°
And that same eye whose bend° doth awe the world
Did lose his° luster; I did hear him groan;

129    **temper:** physical makeup.

130–131    **So get the . . . alone:** get ahead of all others and carry the victor's prize himself.

136    **Colossus:** The Colossus of Rhodes, a gigantic statue of the Greek god Apollo straddling the harbor of Rhodes, was said to be so tall that ships could sail through its legs.

140    **stars:** fate (believed to be determined by the position of the stars and planets at someone's birth).

145    **Sound them:** say them.
146    **conjure:** call up spirits.

150    **Age:** the present era.

152    **great flood:** a time, according to Roman mythology, when a god let loose a flood that drowned all but two people.
153    **But it was . . . man:** That was not celebrated for more than one great man.

156    **Now is it . . . enough:** Cassius makes a pun on the words *Rome* and *room*, which were sometimes pronounced alike in Shakespeare's time.

159–161    **There was . . . king:** There once was a Brutus who would have accepted the devil ruling in Rome as easily as a king. (Cassius refers to Lucius Junius Brutus, who expelled the king of Rome and helped make it a republic in 509 B.C. Brutus claimed this hero as his ancestor.)

| 125 | Ay, and that tongue of his that bade the Romans |
| | Mark him, and write his speeches in their books, |
| | Alas, it cried, "Give me some drink, Titinius," |
| | As a sick girl. Ye gods, it doth amaze me |
| | A man of such a feeble temper° should |
| 130 | So get the start of the majestic world, |
| | And bear the palm alone.° |

[*Shout. Flourish.*]

**BRUTUS.** Another general shout?
    I do believe that these applauses are
    For some new honors that are heap'd on Caesar.

135   **CASSIUS.** Why, man, he doth bestride the narrow world
    Like a Colossus,° and we petty men
    Walk under his huge legs, and peep about
    To find ourselves dishonorable graves.
    Men at some time are masters of their fates;
140     The fault, dear Brutus, is not in our stars,°
    But in ourselves, that we are underlings.
    Brutus and Caesar; what should be in that "Caesar"?
    Why should that name be sounded more than yours?
    Write them together, yours is as fair a name;
145     Sound them,° it doth become the mouth as well;
    Weigh them, it is as heavy; conjure° with 'em,
    "Brutus" will start a spirit as soon as "Caesar."
    Now, in the names of all the gods at once,
    Upon what meat doth this our Caesar feed,
150     That he is grown so great? Age,° thou art sham'd!
    Rome, thou hast lost the breed of noble bloods!
    When went there by an age, since the great flood°
    But it was fam'd with more than with one man?°
    When could they say, till now, that talk'd of Rome,
155     That her wide walks encompass'd but one man?
    Now is it Rome indeed and room enough,°
    When there is in it but one only man.
    O! you and I have heard our fathers say
    There was a Brutus once that would have brook'd
160     Th' eternal devil to keep his state in Rome
    As easily as a king.°

162 **am nothing jealous:** have no doubt.
163 **have some aim:** can guess.

167 **mov'd:** urged.

170 **meet:** suitable.
171 **chew:** ponder.

181 **What hath . . . today:** What noteworthy things have occurred today.

184 **chidden train:** scolded band of followers.
185 **Cicero:** a Roman senator famous for his oratory.
186 **ferret:** ferretlike. (The ferret, a member of the weasel family, is known for its ability to flush out and dart after its prey.)

197 **well given:** favorably disposed (toward Caesar).

**BRUTUS.** That you do love me, I am nothing jealous;°
What you would work me to, I have some aim.°
How I have thought of this, and of these times,
165 I shall recount hereafter. For this present,
I would not (so with love I might entreat you)
Be any further mov'd.° What you have said
I will consider; what you have to say
I will with patience hear, and find a time
170 Both meet° to hear and answer such high things.
Till then, my noble friend, chew° upon this;
Brutus had rather be a villager
Than to repute himself a son of Rome
Under these hard conditions as this time
175 Is like to lay upon us.

**CASSIUS.** I am glad that my weak words
Have struck but thus much show of fire from Brutus.

[*Enter* CAESAR *and his* TRAIN.]

**BRUTUS.** The games are done, and Caesar is returning.

**CASSIUS.** As they pass by, pluck Casca by the sleeve,
180 And he will (after his sour fashion) tell you
What hath proceeded worthy note today.°

**BRUTUS.** I will do so. But look you, Cassius,
The angry spot doth glow on Caesar's brow,
And all the rest look like a chidden train;°
185 Calphurnia's cheek is pale, and Cicero°
Looks with such ferret° and such fiery eyes
As we have seen him in the Capitol,
Being cross'd in conference by some senators.

**CASSIUS.** Casca will tell us what the matter is.

190 **CAESAR.** Antonio!

**ANTONY.** Caesar?

**CAESAR.** Let me have men about me that are fat,
Sleek-headed men, and such as sleep a-nights.
Yond Cassius has a lean and hungry look,
195 He thinks too much; such men are dangerous.

**ANTONY.** Fear him not, Caesar, he's not dangerous,
He is a noble Roman, and well given.°

**CAESAR.** Would he were fatter! But I fear him not.

199    **if my name . . . fear:** if it were possible for me to fear anyone.

202–203    **looks . . . of men:** sees people's true motives in their actions.

206–207    **scorn'd . . . any thing:** disdained the impulse that could make him smile at all.

216    **chanc'd:** happened.

217    **sad:** serious.

221    **put it by:** pushed it aside.

228    **marry, was't:** indeed it was.

229    **honest:** worthy (said sarcastically).

Yet if my name were liable to fear,°
200 I do not know the man I should avoid
So soon as that spare Cassius. He reads much,
He is a great observer, and he looks
Quite through the deeds of men.° He loves no plays,
As thou dost, Antony; he hears no music;
205 Seldom he smiles, and smiles in such a sort
As if he mock'd himself, and scorn'd his spirit
That could be mov'd to smile at any thing.°
Such men as he be never at heart's ease
Whiles they behold a greater than themselves,
210 And therefore are they very dangerous.
I rather tell thee what is to be fear'd
Than what I fear; for always I am Caesar.
Come on my right hand, for this ear is deaf,
And tell me truly what thou think'st of him.

[CAESAR *and his* TRAIN *exit.* CASCA *stays.*]

215 CASCA. You pull'd me by the cloak, would you speak with me?

BRUTUS. Ay, Casca; tell us what hath chanc'd° today,
That Caesar looks so sad.°

CASCA. Why, you were with him, were you not?

BRUTUS. I should not then ask Casca what had chanc'd.

220 CASCA. Why, there was a crown offer'd him; and being offer'd
him, he put it by° with the back of his hand, thus, and then
the people fell a-shouting.

BRUTUS. What was the second noise for?

CASCA. Why, for that too.

225 CASSIUS. They shouted thrice; what was the last cry for?

CASCA. Why, for that too.

BRUTUS. Was the crown offer'd him thrice?

CASCA. Ay, marry, was't,° and he put it by thrice, every time
gentler than other; and at every putting-by mine honest°
230 neighbors shouted.

CASSIUS. Who offer'd him the crown?

CASCA. Why, Antony.

BRUTUS. Tell us the manner of it, gentle Casca.

235  **mark:** pay attention to.

237  **coronets:** ornamental wreaths or headbands.
238  **fain:** gladly.

243  **chopp'd:** chapped.

246  **swounded:** fainted.

249  **soft:** wait a minute.

252  **'Tis very . . . falling sickness:** It's very likely that he has epilepsy.

256  **tag-rag people:** ragged mob.

261–262  **pluck'd . . . doublet:** ripped open his short jacket.
262–263  **And I . . . occupation:** If I had been "a man of action" (or "a laborer").
264  **a word:** his word.

**CASCA.** I can as well be hang'd as tell the manner of it; it was
mere foolery, I did not mark° it. I saw Mark Antony offer
him a crown—yet 'twas not a crown neither, 'twas one of
these coronets°—and as I told you, he put it by once; but
for all that, to my thinking, he would fain° have had it.
Then he offer'd it to him again; then he put it by again; but
to my thinking, he was very loath to lay his fingers off it.
And then he offer'd it the third time; he put it the third
time by; and still as he refus'd it, the rabblement hooted,
and clapp'd their chopp'd° hands, and threw up their sweaty
nightcaps, and utter'd such a deal of stinking breath because Caesar refus'd the crown, that it had, almost, chok'd
Caesar; for he swounded,° and fell down at it; and for mine
own part, I durst not laugh, for fear of opening my lips and
receiving the bad air.

**CASSIUS.** But, soft,° I pray you; what, did Caesar swound?

**CASCA.** He fell down in the market place, and foam'd at
mouth, and was speechless.

**BRUTUS.** 'Tis very like, he hath the falling sickness.°

**CASSIUS.** No, Caesar hath it not; but you, and I,
And honest Casca, we have the falling sickness.

**CASCA.** I know not what you mean by that, but I am sure
Caesar fell down. If the tag-rag people° did not clap him
and hiss him, according as he pleas'd and displeas'd them,
as they use to do the players in the theater, I am no true man.

**BRUTUS.** What said he when he came unto himself?

**CASCA.** Marry, before he fell down, when he perceiv'd the
common herd was glad he refus'd the crown, he pluck'd me
ope his doublet,° and offer'd them his throat to cut. And I
had been a man of any occupation,° if I would not have
taken him at a word,° I would I might go to hell among the
rogues. And so he fell. When he came to himself again, he
said, if he had done or said anything amiss, he desir'd their
worships to think it was his infirmity. Three or four wenches,
where I stood, cried, "Alas, good soul!" and forgave
him with all their hearts. But there's no heed to be taken of
them; if Caesar had stabb'd their mothers, they would have
done no less.

**BRUTUS.** And after that, he came thus sad away?

279–280    **it was Greek to me:** I couldn't understand a word of it.

281    **put to silence:** removed from office.

286    **your mind hold:** you don't change your mind.

291    **quick mettle:** lively, clever.

294    **However . . . form:** Although he puts on this dull manner.

296    **disgest:** digest.

302    **the world:** the present state of affairs.

304–305    **Thy honorable . . . dispos'd:** Your honorable nature can be manipulated to go against its normal inclinations.

305    **meet:** appropriate.

308    **doth bear me hard:** dislikes me.

CASCA.  Ay.

CASSIUS.  Did Cicero say anything?

275 CASCA.  Ay, he spoke Greek.

CASSIUS.  To what effect?

CASCA.  Nay, and I tell you that, I'll ne'er look you i' th' face
again. But those that understood him smil'd at one another,
and shook their heads; but for mine own part, it was Greek
280 to me.° I could tell you more news too; Murellus and Flavius,
for pulling scarfs off Caesar's images, are put to silence.° Fare
you well. There was more foolery yet, if I could remember it.

CASSIUS.  Will you sup with me tonight, Casca?

CASCA.  No, I am promis'd forth.

285 CASSIUS.  Will you dine with me tomorrow?

CASCA.  Ay, if I be alive, and your mind hold,° and your dinner
worth the eating.

CASSIUS.  Good, I will expect you.

CASCA.  Do so. Farewell, both. [Exit.]

290 BRUTUS.  What a blunt fellow is this grown to be!
He was quick mettle° when he went to school.

CASSIUS.  So is he now in execution
Of any bold or noble enterprise,
However he puts on this tardy form.°
295 This rudeness is a sauce to his good wit,
Which gives men stomach to disgest° his words
With better appetite.

BRUTUS.  And so it is. For this time I will leave you.
Tomorrow, if you please to speak with me,
300 I will come home to you, or, if you will,
Come home to me, and I will wait for you.

CASSIUS.  I will do so. Till then, think of the world.°

[Exit BRUTUS.]

Well, Brutus, thou art noble; yet I see
Thy honorable mettle may be wrought
305 From that it is dispos'd;° therefore it is meet°
That noble minds keep ever with their likes;
For who so firm that cannot be seduc'd?
Caesar doth bear me hard,° but he loves Brutus.

310    **humor:** influence.

310–315    **I will . . . glanced at:** Tonight I will throw letters in different handwriting, as if they came from several citizens, into Brutus's windows. The letters will relate that Brutus is highly regarded in Rome and will subtly hint at Caesar's ambition.

316    **seat him sure:** seat himself securely.

1    **even:** evening.

3    **sway:** realm.

6    **riv'd:** split.

8    **exalted with:** raised as high as.

12    **saucy:** insolent.

18    **sensible of:** sensitive to.

21    **glaz'd:** stared.

22–23    **drawn . . . heap:** huddled together.

26    **bird of night:** screech owl.

If I were Brutus now and he were Cassius,
310 He should not humor° me. I will this night,
In several hands, in at his windows throw,
As if they came from several citizens,
Writings, all tending to the great opinion
That Rome holds of his name; wherein obscurely
315 Caesar's ambition shall be glanced at.°
And after this, let Caesar seat him sure,°
For we will shake him, or worse days endure. [*Exit.*]


## SCENE 3. A Roman street. One month later.

[*Thunder and lightning. Enter (from opposite sides)* CASCA (*with his sword drawn*) *and* CICERO.]

**CICERO.**  Good even,° Casca; brought you Caesar home?
Why are you breathless? And why stare you so?

**CASCA.**  Are not you mov'd, when all the sway° of earth
Shakes like a thing unfirm? O Cicero,
5 I have seen tempests, when the scolding winds
Have riv'd° the knotty oaks, and I have seen
Th' ambitious ocean swell and rage and foam,
To be exalted with° the threat'ning clouds;
But never till tonight, never till now,
10 Did I go through a tempest dropping fire.
Either there is a civil strife in heaven,
Or else the world, too saucy° with the gods,
Incenses them to send destruction.

**CICERO.**  Why, saw you any thing more wonderful?

15 **CASCA.**  A common slave—you know him well by sight—
Held up his left hand, which did flame and burn
Like twenty torches join'd; and yet his hand,
Not sensible of° fire, remain'd unscorch'd.
Besides—I ha' not since put up my sword—
20 Against the Capitol I met a lion,
Who glaz'd° upon me and went surly by,
Without annoying me. And there were drawn
Upon a heap° a hundred ghastly women,
Transformed with their fear, who swore they saw
25 Men, all in fire, walk up and down the streets.
And yesterday the bird of night° did sit

28   **prodigies:**  bizarre events.

29   **conjointly meet:**  coincide.

31–32   **portentous . . . point upon:**  bad omens for the place where they occur.

34–35   **But men may . . . themselves:**  But people may interpret things in their own way, regardless of the real meaning of the things.

42   **what night is this:**  what a night this is!

47   **Submitting me:**  exposing myself.

48   **unbraced:**  with jacket open.

49   **thunder-stone:**  thunderbolt.

52   **in the aim:**  at the point where it was directed.

55   **tokens:**  ominous signs.

56   **astonish:**  stun with fear.

57   **dull:**  stupid.

58   **want:**  lack.

Even at noonday upon the marketplace,
Hooting and shrieking. When these prodigies°
Do so conjointly meet,° let not men say,

30 "These are their reasons, they are natural";
For I believe they are portentous things
Unto the climate that they point upon.°

CICERO. Indeed, it is a strange-disposed time;
But men may construe things after their fashion,

35 Clean from the purpose of the things themselves.°
Comes Caesar to the Capitol tomorrow?

CASCA. He doth; for he did bid Antonio
Send word to you he would be there tomorrow.

CICERO. Good night then, Casca; this disturbed sky

40 Is not to walk in.

CASCA.                     Farewell, Cicero.    [*Exit* CICERO.]

[*Enter* CASSIUS.]

CASSIUS. Who's there?

CASCA.                     A Roman.

CASSIUS.                               Casca, by your voice.

CASCA. Your ear is good. Cassius, what night is this!°

CASSIUS. A very pleasing night to honest men.

CASCA. Who ever knew the heavens menace so?

45 CASSIUS. Those that have known the earth so full of faults.
For my part, I have walk'd about the streets,
Submitting me° unto the perilous night;
And thus unbraced,° Casca, as you see,
Have bar'd my bosom to the thunder-stone;°

50 And when the cross blue lightning seem'd to open
The breast of heaven, I did present myself
Even in the aim° and very flash of it.

CASCA. But wherefore did you so much tempt the heavens?
It is the part of men to fear and tremble

55 When the most mighty gods by tokens° send
Such dreadful heralds to astonish° us.

CASSIUS. You are dull,° Casca; and those sparks of life
That should be in a Roman you do want,°
Or else you use not. You look pale, and gaze,

| 64 | **from quality and kind:** (act) contrary to their nature. |
| 65 | **calculate:** make prophecies. |

| 66–71 | **Why all these . . . state:** Cassius argues that things have changed from their normal behavior as a heavenly warning of some unnatural state of affairs. |

| 77–78 | **yet prodigious . . . fearful:** yet has become ominous and threatening. |

| 81 | **thews:** muscles. |
| 82 | **woe the while:** alas for these times. |

| 84 | **yoke and sufferance:** servitude and patient submission. |

| 89–90 | **I know . . . deliver Cassius:** Cassius says that he would rather kill himself than submit to Caesar. |
| 91 | **Therein:** in that way (referring to suicide). |

| | |
|---|---|
| 60 | And put on fear, and cast yourself in wonder, |
| | To see the strange impatience of the heavens; |
| | But if you would consider the true cause |
| | Why all these fires, why all these gliding ghosts, |
| | Why birds and beasts from quality and kind,° |
| 65 | Why old men, fools, and children calculate,° |
| | Why all these things change from their ordinance, |
| | Their natures and preformed faculties, |
| | To monstrous quality—why, you shall find |
| | That heaven hath infus'd them with these spirits, |
| 70 | To make them instruments of fear and warning |
| | Unto some monstrous state.° |
| | Now could I, Casca, name to thee a man |
| | Most like this dreadful night, |
| | That thunders, lightens, opens graves, and roars |
| 75 | As doth the lion in the Capitol— |
| | A man no mightier than thyself, or me, |
| | In personal action, yet prodigious grown |
| | And fearful,° as these strange eruptions are. |

CASCA.   'Tis Caesar that you mean; is it not, Cassius?

|  |  |
|---|---|
| 80 | CASSIUS.   Let it be who it is; for Romans now |
| | Have thews° and limbs like to their ancestors; |
| | But, woe the while,° our fathers' minds are dead, |
| | And we are govern'd with our mothers' spirits; |
| | Our yoke and sufferance° show us womanish. |

|  |  |
|---|---|
| 85 | CASCA.   Indeed, they say, the senators tomorrow |
| | Mean to establish Caesar as a king; |
| | And he shall wear his crown by sea and land, |
| | In every place, save here in Italy. |

|  |  |
|---|---|
| | CASSIUS.   I know where I will wear this dagger then; |
| 90 | Cassius from bondage will deliver Cassius.° |
| | Therein,° ye gods, you make the weak most strong; |
| | Therein, ye gods, you tyrants do defeat; |
| | Nor stony tower, nor walls of beaten brass, |
| | Nor airless dungeon, nor strong links of iron, |
| 95 | Can be retentive to the strength of spirit; |
| | But life, being weary of these worldly bars, |
| | Never lacks power to dismiss itself. |
| | If I know this, know all the world besides, |
| | That part of tyranny that I do bear |

106    **hinds:** female deer; servants.

108    **trash:** twigs or garbage.
109    **offal:** chips of wood or garbage.
110    **base matter:** kindling.

112–114    **I, perhaps . . . be made:** Perhaps I am speaking to one who accepts his slavery; if so, I shall have to answer for my words (suggesting that Casca might inform on him).
117    **fleering:** sneering.
118    **Be factious . . . griefs:** Form a group to straighten out all these problems.

121    **mov'd:** persuaded.

125–126    **by this . . . Porch:** By this time they wait for me in the entrance to the theater built by Pompey.

128–129    **the complexion . . . in hand:** The condition of the sky appears similar to the work we have to do.

131    **close:** concealed.

100      I can shake off at pleasure.

[*Thunder still.*]

> CASCA.                 So can I;
> So every bondman in his own hand bears
> The power to cancel his captivity.

> CASSIUS.    And why should Caesar be a tyrant then?
> Poor man, I know he would not be a wolf,
> 105     But that he sees the Romans are but sheep;
> He were no lion, were not Romans hinds.°
> Those that with haste will make a mighty fire
> Begin it with weak straws. What trash° is Rome?
> What rubbish and what offal?° when it serves
> 110    For the base matter° to illuminate
> So vile a thing as Caesar! But, O grief,
> Where hast thou led me? I, perhaps, speak this
> Before a willing bondman; then I know
> My answer must be made.° But I am arm'd,
> 115    And dangers are to me indifferent.

> CASCA.    You speak to Casca, and to such a man
> That is no fleering° tell-tale. Hold, my hand.
> Be factious for redress of all these griefs,°
> And I will set this foot of mine as far
> 120    As who goes farthest.

> CASSIUS.               There's a bargain made.
> Now know you, Casca, I have mov'd° already
> Some certain of the noblest-minded Romans
> To undergo with me an enterprise
> Of honorable-dangerous consequence;
> 125    And I do know, by this they stay for me
> In Pompey's Porch;° for now, this fearful night,
> There is no stir or walking in the streets;
> And the complexion of the element
> [In] favor's like the work we have in hand,°
> 130    Most bloody, fiery, and most terrible.

[*Enter* CINNA.]

> CASCA.    Stand close° awhile, for here comes one in haste.

> CASSIUS.    'Tis Cinna, I do know him by his gait,
> He is a friend. Cinna, where haste you so?

135 **incorporate:** joined.

136 **stayed for:** awaited.

137 **on't:** of it.

142–146 **Good Cinna . . . statue:** Marcus Brutus held the office of praetor, a high-ranking judge who settled disputes brought before him. Cassius directs Cinna to leave one letter on Brutus's chair, throw a second into his window, and fasten a third onto the statue of the hero Lucius Junius Brutus.

147 **Repair:** go.

150 **hie:** hurry.

155–156 **the man . . . ours:** When we next meet him, he will be entirely in our hands.

159–160 **His countenance . . . worthiness:** Alchemy was the "science" of trying to turn base metals into gold. Casca says that Brutus's noble reputation will change the public's attitude toward their plot from condemnation to admiration.

162 **conceited:** understood.

**CINNA.**  To find out you. Who's that? Metellus Cimber?

135 **CASSIUS.**  No, it is Casca, one incorporate°
 To our attempts. Am I not stay'd for,° Cinna?

**CINNA.**  I am glad on't.° What a fearful night is this!
 There's two or three of us have seen strange sights.

**CASSIUS.**  Am I not stay'd for? tell me.

**CINNA.**                                          Yes, you are.
140 O Cassius, if you could
 But win the noble Brutus to our party—

**CASSIUS.**  Be you content. Good Cinna, take this paper,
 And look you lay it in the praetor's chair,
 Where Brutus may but find it; and throw this
145 In at his window; set this up with wax
 Upon old Brutus' statue.° All this done,
 Repair° to Pompey's Porch, where you shall find us.
 Is Decius Brutus and Trebonius there?

**CINNA.**  All but Metellus Cimber, and he's gone
150 To seek you at your house. Well, I will hie,°
 And so bestow these papers as you bade me.

**CASSIUS.**  That done, repair to Pompey's theater.

[*Exit* CINNA.]

 Come, Casca, you and I will yet ere day
 See Brutus at his house. Three parts of him
155 Is ours already, and the man entire
 Upon the next encounter yields him ours.°

**CASCA.**  O, he sits high in all the people's hearts;
 And that which would appear offense in us,
 His countenance, like richest alchemy,
160 Will change to virtue and to worthiness.°

**CASSIUS.**  Him, and his worth, and our great need of him,
 You have right well conceited.° Let us go,
 For it is after midnight, and ere day
 We will awake him and be sure of him.

[*They exit.*]

2    **progress:** position.

4    **I would . . . fault:** I wish it were my weakness.

7    **taper:** candle.

10    **his death:** Caesar's death.
11    **spurn:** strike out.
12    **the general:** the public good.

14    **adder:** poisonous snake.
15    **craves:** demands; **that:** king or emperor.

18–19    **Th' abuse . . . power:** Greatness is misused when it separates compassion
         from power.
20    **affections sway'd:** desires ruled.
21    **proof:** experience.
22    **lowliness:** humility.

# Act 2

**SCENE 1.** BRUTUS's garden. The ides of March.

[*Enter BRUTUS in his orchard.*]

    **BRUTUS.**   What, Lucius, ho!
     I cannot, by the progress° of the stars,
     Give guess how near to day. Lucius, I say!
     I would it were my fault° to sleep so soundly.
5     When, Lucius, when? Awake, I say! What, Lucius!

[*Enter LUCIUS.*]

    **LUCIUS.**   Call'd you, my lord?

    **BRUTUS.**   Get me a taper° in my study, Lucius.
     When it is lighted, come and call me here.

    **LUCIUS.**   I will, my lord.

[*Exit LUCIUS.*]

10  **BRUTUS.**   It must be by his death;° and for my part,
     I know no personal cause to spurn° at him,
     But for the general.° He would be crown'd:
     How that might change his nature, there's the question.
     It is the bright day that brings forth the adder,°
15     And that craves° wary walking. Crown him that,°
     And then I grant we put a sting in him
     That at his will he may do danger with.
     Th' abuse of greatness is when it disjoins
     Remorse from power;° and, to speak truth of Caesar,
20     I have not known when his affections sway'd°
     More than his reason. But 'tis a common proof°
     That lowliness° is young ambition's ladder,
     Whereto the climber-upward turns his face;

24 **upmost round:** top rung.

28 **lest . . . prevent:** For fear that he may, let us prevent it.

28–31 **since the quarrel . . . extremities:** Since our complaints are not supported by Caesar's present behavior, we will have to put our case the following way: if given more power, Caesar's nature would lead him to such and such extremes.

35 **closet:** small private room.

44 **exhalations:** meteors.

47 **redress:** correct a wrong.

49 **instigations:** letters urging action.

51 **piece it out:** fill in the gaps in meaning.

54 **Tarquin:** (tär' kwin) the last king of Rome, driven out by Lucius Junius Brutus.

55–58 **Speak, strike . . . Brutus:** Brutus vows that Rome's petition for redress will be granted if it can be done through his words and actions.

But when he once attains the upmost round,°
25 He then unto the ladder turns his back,
Looks in the clouds, scorning the base degrees
By which he did ascend. So Caesar may;
Then lest he may, prevent.° And since the quarrel
Will bear no color for the thing he is,
30 Fashion it thus: that what he is, augmented,
Would run to these and these extremities;°
And therefore think him as a serpent's egg,
Which hatch'd, would as his kind grow mischievous,
And kill him in the shell.

[*Enter* LUCIUS.]

35 **LUCIUS.** The taper burneth in your closet,° sir.
Searching the window for a flint, I found
This paper thus seal'd up, and I am sure
It did not lie there when I went to bed.

[*Gives him the letter.*]

**BRUTUS.** Get you to bed again, it is not day.
40 Is not tomorrow, boy, the [ides] of March?

**LUCIUS.** I know not, sir.

**BRUTUS.** Look in the calendar, and bring me word.

**LUCIUS.** I will, sir. [*Exit.*]

**BRUTUS.** The exhalations° whizzing in the air
45 Give so much light that I may read by them.

[*Opens the letter and reads.*]

"Brutus, thou sleep'st; awake, and see thyself!
Shall Rome, etc. Speak, strike, redress!"°
"Brutus, thou sleep'st; awake."
Such instigations° have been often dropp'd
50 Where I have took them up.
"Shall Rome, etc." Thus must I piece it out:°
Shall Rome stand under one man's awe? What, Rome?
My ancestors did from the streets of Rome
The Tarquin° drive when he was call'd a king.
55 "Speak, strike, redress!" Am I entreated
To speak and strike? O Rome, I make thee promise,
If the redress will follow, thou receivest
Thy full petition at the hand of Brutus!°

[*Enter* LUCIUS.]

61    **whet:** incite.

64    **motion:** prompting.

65    **phantasma:** nightmare.

66    **Genius . . . instruments:** the mental and physical powers that allow some-one to take action.

67–69    **the state . . . insurrection:** Brutus compares his conflicted state of mind to a kingdom paralyzed by civil unrest.

70    **brother:** brother-in-law. (Cassius is married to Brutus's sister, Junia.)

72    **moe:** more.

75    **discover:** identify.

76    **favor:** appearance.

78    **Sham'st thou:** Are you ashamed?

83    **path . . . semblance:** go about undisguised.

84    **Erebus:** (er′ ə bəs) in classical mythology, the dark place through which the dead pass on their way to Hades, the underworld.

85    **prevention:** discovery and being thwarted.

86    **too bold upon:** intruding upon too presumptuously.

87    **morrow:** morning.

LUCIUS.   Sir, March is wasted fifteen days.

[*Knock within.*]

60    BRUTUS.   'Tis good. Go to the gate, somebody knocks.

[*Exit LUCIUS.*]
          Since Cassius first did whet° me against Caesar,
          I have not slept.
          Between the acting of a dreadful thing
          And the first motion,° all the interim is
65        Like a phantasma,° or a hideous dream.
          The Genius and the mortal instruments°
          Are then in council, and the state of a man,
          Like to a little kingdom, suffers then
          The nature of an insurrection.°

[*Enter LUCIUS.*]

70    LUCIUS.   Sir, 'tis your brother° Cassius at the door,
          Who doth desire to see you.

      BRUTUS.                              Is he alone?

      LUCIUS.   No, sir, there are moe° with him.

      BRUTUS.                                        Do you know them?

      LUCIUS.   No, sir; their hats are pluck'd about their ears,
          And half their faces buried in their cloaks,
75        That by no means I may discover° them
          By any mark of favor.°

      BRUTUS.                    Let 'em enter.

[*Exit LUCIUS.*]
          They are the faction. O Conspiracy,
          Sham'st thou° to show thy dang'rous brow by night,
          When evils are most free? O then, by day
80        Where wilt thou find a cavern dark enough
          To mask thy monstrous visage? Seek none, Conspiracy;
          Hide it in smiles and affability;
          For if thou path, thy native semblance° on,
          Not Erebus° itself were dim enough
85        To hide thee from prevention.°

[*Enter the CONSPIRATORS, CASSIUS, CASCA, DECIUS, CINNA, METELLUS, and TREBONIUS.*]

      CASSIUS.   I think we are too bold upon° your rest.
          Good morrow,° Brutus, do we trouble you?

**What watchful . . . night:** What worries keep you awake?

104    **fret:** interlace.

106–111    **Here, as I . . . directly here:** Casca insists that in the early spring the sun rises south of the spot pointed out by Decius and Cinna; it will rise farther north in about two months.

112    **all over:** all of you.

114–116    **If not . . . betimes:** The sadness in people's faces, the suffering of our souls, the corruption of our age—if these are weak motives, let's give up at once.

118    **high-sighted:** arrogant.

119    **drop by lottery:** die by chance (at Caesar's whim).

120    **bear fire:** are spirited.

**BRUTUS.**   I have been up this hour, awake all night.
Know I these men that come along with you?

90  **CASSIUS.**   Yes, every man of them; and no man here
But honors you; and every one doth wish
You had but that opinion of yourself
Which every noble Roman bears of you.
This is Trebonius.

**BRUTUS.**                    He is welcome hither.

95  **CASSIUS.**   This, Decius Brutus.

**BRUTUS.**                         He is welcome too.

**CASSIUS.**   This, Casca; this, Cinna; and this, Metellus Cimber.

**BRUTUS.**   They are all welcome.
What watchful cares do interpose themselves
Betwixt your eyes and night?°

100  **CASSIUS.**   Shall I entreat a word?

[*They whisper.*]

**DECIUS.**   Here lies the east; doth not the day break here?

**CASCA.**   No.

**CINNA.**   O, pardon, sir, it doth; and yon gray lines
That fret° the clouds are messengers of day.

105  **CASCA.**   You shall confess that you are both deceiv'd.
Here, as I point my sword, the sun arises,
Which is a great way growing on the south,
Weighing the youthful season of the year.
Some two months hence, up higher toward the north
110  He first presents his fire, and the high east
Stands, as the Capitol, directly here.°

**BRUTUS.**   Give me your hands all over,° one by one.

**CASSIUS.**   And let us swear our resolution.

**BRUTUS.**   No, not an oath. If not the face of men,
115  The sufferance of our souls, the time's abuse—
If these be motives weak, break off betimes,°
And every man hence to his idle bed.
So let high-sighted° tyranny range on
Till each man drop by lottery.° But if these
120  (As I am sure they do) bear fire° enough
To kindle cowards and to steel with valor

124    **prick:** spur.

126    **palter:** waver; deceive.

126–128    **what other oath . . . for it:** What other oath is needed than that of honest men who have pledged to each other that they will prevail or die trying?

129    **cautelous:** wary; crafty.

130    **carrions:** men no better than corpses.

132–136    **do not stain . . . oath:** Do not insult the steadfast virtue of our undertaking or the indomitable courage of our spirits to think that either our cause or our actions require an oath.

136–140    **every drop . . . from him:** Brutus claims that no one of true Roman blood would break a promise.

138    **Is guilty . . . bastardy:** is illegitimate.

141    **sound him:** find out his feelings.

148    **no whit:** not in the least.

149    **gravity:** dignity.

150    **break with him:** reveal our plot to him.

158    **means:** abilities.

The melting spirits of women, then, countrymen,
What need we any spur but our own cause
To prick° us to redress? What other bond
Than secret Romans that have spoke the word
And will not palter?° and what other oath
Than honesty to honesty engag'd
That this shall be, or we will fall for it?°
Swear priests and cowards and men cautelous,°
Old feeble carrions,° and such suffering souls
That welcome wrongs; unto bad causes swear
Such creatures as men doubt; but do not stain
The even virtue of our enterprise,
Nor th' insuppressive mettle of our spirits,
To think that or our cause or our performance
Did need an oath;° when every drop of blood
That every Roman bears, and nobly bears,
Is guilty of a several bastardy,°
If he do break the smallest particle
Of any promise that hath pass'd from him.°

125
130
135
140

CASSIUS.   But what of Cicero? Shall we sound him?°
I think he will stand very strong with us.

CASCA.   Let us not leave him out.

CINNA.                              No, by no means.

METELLUS.   O, let us have him, for his silver hairs
Will purchase us a good opinion,
And buy men's voices to commend our deeds.
It shall be said his judgment rul'd our hands;
Our youths and wildness shall no whit° appear,
But all be buried in his gravity.°

145

BRUTUS.   O, name him not! Let us not break with him,°
For he will never follow anything
That other men begin.

150

CASSIUS.                    Then leave him out.

CASCA.   Indeed, he is not fit.

DECIUS.   Shall no man else be touch'd but only Caesar?

CASSIUS.   Decius, well urg'd. I think it is not meet
Mark Antony, so well belov'd of Caesar,
Should outlive Caesar; we shall find of him
A shrewd contriver; and you know, his means,°

155

159    **improve them:** uses them fully.

160    **annoy:** harm.

164    **Like wrath . . . afterwards:** as if the killings were motivated by anger and malice.

167    **the spirit of Caesar:** what Caesar represents.

169    **come by:** get possession of.

176    **servants:** hands.

184    **ingrafted:** deep-rooted.

187    **take thought and die:** die from grief.

188    **that were much he should:** It is unlikely that he would do such a thing.

190    **no fear in him:** nothing to fear from him.

160　If he improve them,° may well stretch so far
　　　As to annoy° us all; which to prevent,
　　　Let Antony and Caesar fall together.

　　**BRUTUS.**　Our course will seem too bloody, Caius Cassius,
　　　To cut the head off and then hack the limbs—
　　　Like wrath in death and envy afterwards;°
165　For Antony is but a limb of Caesar.
　　　Let's be sacrificers, but not butchers, Caius.
　　　We all stand up against the spirit of Caesar,°
　　　And in the spirit of men there is no blood.
　　　O that we then could come by° Caesar's spirit,
170　And not dismember Caesar! But, alas,
　　　Caesar must bleed for it. And, gentle friends,
　　　Let's kill him boldly, but not wrathfully;
　　　Let's carve him as a dish fit for the gods,
　　　Not hew him as a carcass fit for hounds;
175　And let our hearts, as subtle masters do,
　　　Stir up their servants° to an act of rage,
　　　And after seem to chide 'em. This shall make
　　　Our purpose necessary, and not envious;
　　　Which so appearing to the common eyes,
180　We shall be call'd purgers, not murderers.
　　　And for Mark Antony, think not of him;
　　　For he can do no more than Caesar's arm
　　　When Caesar's head is off.

　　**CASSIUS.**　　　　　　　　　　Yet I fear him,
　　　For in the ingrafted° love he bears to Caesar—

185　**BRUTUS.**　Alas, good Cassius, do not think of him.
　　　If he love Caesar, all that he can do
　　　Is to himself—take thought and die° for Caesar.
　　　And that were much he should,° for he is given
　　　To sports, to wildness, and much company.

190　**TREBONIUS.**　There is no fear in him;° let him not die,
　　For he will live and laugh at this hereafter.

[*Clock strikes.*]

　　**BRUTUS.**　Peace, count the clock.

　　**CASSIUS.**　　　　　　　　　　The clock hath stricken three.

　　**TREBONIUS.**　'Tis time to part.

　　**CASSIUS.**　　　　　　　　　But it is doubtful yet

| | |
|---|---|
| 196 | **Quite from the main opinion:** contrary to the strong opinion. |
| 197 | **ceremonies:** omens. |

| | |
|---|---|
| 200 | **augurers:** religious officials who interpreted omens to predict future events. |

| | |
|---|---|
| 203–206 | **for he loves . . . flatterers:** Decius refers to legends that the mythical unicorn could be tricked into charging a tree and getting its horn stuck, and that bears can be lured by mirrors. He also refers to trapping elephants in pits, using nets to catch lions, and tricking men with flattery. |
| 210 | **give his . . . bent:** put him in the right mood. |

| | |
|---|---|
| 213 | **uttermost:** latest. |

| | |
|---|---|
| 215 | **bear Caesar hard:** strongly resents Caesar. |
| 216 | **rated:** rebuked. |

| | |
|---|---|
| 220 | **fashion:** persuade. |

| | |
|---|---|
| 224–227 | **look fresh . . . constancy:** Brutus warns the others not to let their serious expressions show their intentions; they should carry out their plot appearing at ease and dignified. |

Whether Caesar will come forth today or no;
195     For he is superstitious grown of late,
Quite from the main opinion° he held once
Of fantasy, of dreams, and ceremonies.°
It may be these apparent prodigies,
The unaccustom'd terror of this night,
200     And the persuasion of his augurers°
May hold him from the Capitol today.

DECIUS.    Never fear that. If he be so resolv'd,
I can o'ersway him; for he loves to hear
That unicorns may be betray'd with trees,
205     And bears with glasses, elephants with holes,
Lions with toils, and men with flatterers;°
But when I tell him he hates flatterers
He says he does, being then most flattered.
Let me work;
210     For I can give his humor the true bent,°
And I will bring him to the Capitol.

CASSIUS.    Nay, we will all of us be there to fetch him.

BRUTUS.    By the eight hour; is that the uttermost?°

CINNA.    Be that the uttermost, and fail not then.

215  METELLUS.    Caius Ligarius doth bear Caesar hard,°
Who rated° him for speaking well of Pompey.
I wonder none of you have thought of him.

BRUTUS.    Now, good Metellus, go along by him.
He loves me well, and I have given him reasons;
220     Send him but hither, and I'll fashion° him.

CASSIUS.    The morning comes upon 's; we'll leave you, Brutus.
And, friends, disperse yourselves; but all remember
What you have said, and show yourselves true Romans.

BRUTUS.    Good gentlemen, look fresh and merrily;
225     Let not our looks put on our purposes,
But bear it as our Roman actors do,
With untir'd spirits and formal constancy.°
And so good morrow to you every one.

[*They exit. BRUTUS remains.*]

Boy! Lucius! Fast asleep? It is no matter,
230     Enjoy the honey-heavy dew of slumber.
Thou hast no figures nor no fantasies,

237    **ungently:** discourteously.

240    **across:** folded.

246    **wafter:** waving.

249    **withal:** besides.
250    **but an . . . humor:** only a passing mood.
251    **his:** its.

253–255    **And could . . . Brutus:** And if it could change your appearance as much as it has changed your state of mind, I would not recognize you as Brutus.

261    **physical:** healthy.

262–263    **humors . . . morning:** damp morning mist.

266    **tempt the . . . air:** risk the damp and impure air. (It was believed that the night air was dangerous to breathe because it wasn't purified by the sun's rays.)
268    **sick offense:** harmful disorder.

Which busy care draws in the brains of men;
Therefore thou sleep'st so sound.

[*Enter* PORTIA.]

**PORTIA.**                                         Brutus, my lord!

**BRUTUS.**    Portia! what mean you? wherefore rise you now?
235     It is not for your health thus to commit
        Your weak condition to the raw cold morning.

**PORTIA.**    Nor for yours neither. Y'have ungently,° Brutus,
        Stole from my bed; and yesternight at supper
        You suddenly arose and walk'd about,
240     Musing and sighing, with your arms across;°
        And when I ask'd you what the matter was,
        You star'd upon me with ungentle looks.
        I urg'd you further; then you scratch'd your head,
        And too impatiently stamp'd with your foot.
245     Yet I insisted, yet you answer'd not,
        But with an angry wafter° of your hand
        Gave sign for me to leave you. So I did,
        Fearing to strengthen that impatience
        Which seem'd too much enkindled, and withal°
250     Hoping it was but an effect of humor,°
        Which sometimes hath his° hour with every man.
        It will not let you eat, nor talk, nor sleep,
        And could it work so much upon your shape
        As it hath much prevail'd on your condition,
255     I should not know you Brutus.° Dear my lord,
        Make me acquainted with your cause of grief.

**BRUTUS.**    I am not well in health, and that is all.

**PORTIA.**    Brutus is wise and, were he not in health,
        He would embrace the means to come by it.

260  **BRUTUS.**    Why, so I do. Good Portia, go to bed.

**PORTIA.**    Is Brutus sick, and is it physical°
        To walk unbraced and suck up the humors
        Of the dank morning?° What, is Brutus sick,
        And will he steal out of his wholesome bed,
265     To dare the vile contagion of the night,
        And tempt the rheumy and unpurged air°
        To add unto his sickness? No, my Brutus;
        You have some sick offense° within your mind,

269    **by the right . . . place:** as your wife.

283    **in sort or limitation:** after a fashion or within limits.

285    **suburbs:** outskirts.

295    **Cato's daughter:** Portia's father, Marcus Porcius Cato, killed himself rather than submit to Caesar's rule after Pompey was defeated.

299–301    **I have made . . . thigh:** Portia reveals that she intentionally cut her thigh before approaching Brutus to show her strong determination.

Which by the right and virtue of my place,°
270    I ought to know of; and upon my knees
I charm you, by my once commended beauty,
By all your vows of love, and that great vow
Which did incorporate and make us one,
That you unfold to me, yourself, your half,
275    Why you are heavy, and what men tonight
Have had resort to you; for here have been
Some six or seven, who did hide their faces
Even from darkness.

**BRUTUS.**                Kneel not, gentle Portia.

**PORTIA.**   I should not need, if you were gentle Brutus.
280    Within the bond of marriage, tell me, Brutus,
Is it excepted I should know no secrets
That appertain to you? Am I your self
But, as it were, in sort or limitation,°
To keep with you at meals, comfort your bed,
285    And talk to you sometimes? Dwell I but in the suburbs°
Of your good pleasure? If it be no more,
Portia is Brutus' harlot, not his wife.

**BRUTUS.**   You are my true and honorable wife,
As dear to me as are the ruddy drops
290    That visit my sad heart.

**PORTIA.**   If this were true, then should I know this secret.
I grant I am a woman; but withal
A woman that Lord Brutus took to wife.
I grant I am a woman; but withal
295    A woman well reputed, Cato's daughter.°
Think you I am no stronger than my sex,
Being so father'd and so husbanded?
Tell me your counsels, I will not disclose 'em.
I have made strong proof of my constancy,
300    Giving myself a voluntary wound
Here, in the thigh;° can I bear that with patience,
And not my husband's secrets?

**BRUTUS.**             O ye gods!
Render me worthy of this noble wife! [*Knock.*]
Hark, hark, one knocks. Portia, go in a while,
305    And by and by thy bosom shall partake
The secrets of my heart.

307 **construe:** explain.

308 **charactery of . . . brows:** what is written in my sad brows (the reasons I am sad).

312 **how:** how are you?

313 **Vouchsafe:** Please accept.

315 **kerchief:** a scarf (wrapped around an ill person's head to protect against drafts).

323 **exorcist:** one who summons up spirits.

324 **mortified:** deadened.

330–331 **I shall . . . done:** They are going to Caesar's house to escort him to the Capitol.

331 **Set on your foot:** Go ahead.

All my engagements I will construe° to thee,
All the charactery of my sad brows.°
Leave me with haste.

[*Exit* PORTIA.]

Lucius, who's that knocks?

[*Enter* LUCIUS *and* CAIUS LIGARIUS.]

310   **LUCIUS.**   Here is a sick man that would speak with you.

**BRUTUS.**   Caius Ligarius, that Metellus spake of.
Boy, stand aside. [*Exit* LUCIUS.] Caius Ligarius, how?°

**CAIUS.**   Vouchsafe° good morrow from a feeble tongue.

**BRUTUS.**   O, what a time have you chose out, brave Caius,
315   To wear a kerchief!° Would you were not sick!

**CAIUS.**   I am not sick, if Brutus have in hand
Any exploit worthy the name of honor.

**BRUTUS.**   Such an exploit have I in hand, Ligarius,
Had you a healthful ear to hear of it.

320   **CAIUS.**   By all the gods that Romans bow before,
I here discard my sickness!
                      Soul of Rome!
Brave son, deriv'd from honorable loins!
Thou, like an exorcist,° hast conjur'd up
My mortified° spirit. Now bid me run,
325   And I will strive with things impossible,
Yea, get the better of them. What's to do?

**BRUTUS.**   A piece of work that will make sick men whole.

**CAIUS.**   But are not some whole that we must make sick?

**BRUTUS.**   That must we also. What it is, my Caius,
330   I shall unfold to thee, as we are going
To whom it must be done.°

**CAIUS.**              Set on your foot.°
And with a heart new-fir'd I follow you,
To do I know not what; but it sufficeth
That Brutus leads me on.

[*Thunder.*]

**BRUTUS.**               Follow me, then. [*They exit.*]

1  **Nor . . . nor:** neither . . . nor.

3  **murther:** murder.

5–6  **Go bid . . . success:** Tell the priests to make a sacrifice immediately, and bring me their interpretations of the results.

13  **stood on ceremonies:** believed in omens.

16  **watch:** night watchmen.
17  **whelped:** given birth.
18  **yawn'd:** opened.

20  **right form of war:** proper military formation.

25  **use:** normal experience.

29  **Are to the . . . Caesar:** apply to everyone as well as to me.

# SCENE 2. CAESAR's house. A few hours later.

[*Thunder and lightning. Enter JULIUS CAESAR in his nightgown.*]

    CAESAR.  Nor heaven nor° earth have been at peace tonight.
       Thrice hath Calphurnia in her sleep cried out,
       "Help, ho! they murther° Caesar!" Who's within?

[*Enter a SERVANT.*]

    SERVANT.  My lord?

5    CAESAR.  Go bid the priests do present sacrifice,
       And bring me their opinions of success.°

    SERVANT.  I will, my lord. [*Exit.*]

[*Enter CALPHURNIA.*]

    CALPHURNIA.  What mean you, Caesar? Think you to walk forth?
       You shall not stir out of your house today.

10    CAESAR.  Caesar shall forth; the things that threaten'd me
       Ne'er look'd but on my back; when they shall see
       The face of Caesar, they are vanished.

    CALPHURNIA.  Caesar, I never stood on ceremonies,°
       Yet now they fright me. There is one within,
15      Besides the things that we have heard and seen,
       Recounts most horrid sights seen by the watch.°
       A lioness hath whelped° in the streets,
       And graves have yawn'd,° and yielded up their dead;
       Fierce fiery warriors fight upon the clouds
20      In ranks and squadrons and right form of war,°
       Which drizzled blood upon the Capitol;
       The noise of battle hurtled in the air;
       Horses did neigh, and dying men did groan,
       And ghosts did shriek and squeal about the streets.
25      O Caesar, these things are beyond all use,°
       And I do fear them.

    CAESAR.            What can be avoided
       Whose end is purpos'd by the mighty gods?
       Yet Caesar shall go forth; for these predictions
       Are to the world in general as to Caesar.°

30    CALPHURNIA.  When beggars die, there are no comets seen;
       The heavens themselves blaze forth the death of princes.

    CAESAR.  Cowards die many times before their deaths,
       The valiant never taste of death but once.

**39–40**    **Plucking the . . . beast:** Augurers would examine the inner organs of a sacrificed animal to predict the future. The absence of a heart would be a strange and unfavorable omen.

**41**    **in shame of:** to shame.

**44–46**    **Danger knows . . . day:** Caesar uses two figures of speech, first personifying danger and then using the metaphor that he and danger are lions born on the same day.

**56**    **humor:** whim.

**60**    **in very happy time:** at the right moment.

Of all the wonders that I yet have heard,
35      It seems to me most strange that men should fear,
Seeing that death, a necessary end,
Will come when it will come.

[*Enter a* SERVANT.]

                                    What say the augurers?

SERVANT.    They would not have you to stir forth today.
Plucking the entrails of an offering forth,
40      They could not find a heart within the beast.°

CAESAR.    The gods do this in shame of° cowardice;
Caesar should be a beast without a heart
If he should stay at home today for fear.
No, Caesar shall not; Danger knows full well
45      That Caesar is more dangerous than he.
We [are] two lions litter'd in one day,°
And I the elder and more terrible;
And Caesar shall go forth.

CALPHURNIA.                          Alas, my lord,
Your wisdom is consum'd in confidence.
50      Do not go forth today; call it my fear
That keeps you in the house and not your own.
We'll send Mark Antony to the Senate House,
And he shall say you are not well today.
Let me, upon my knee, prevail in this.

55      CAESAR.    Mark Antony shall say I am not well,
And for thy humor,° I will stay at home.

[*Enter* DECIUS.]

Here's Decius Brutus, he shall tell them so.

DECIUS.    Caesar, all hail! good morrow, worthy Caesar,
I come to fetch you to the Senate House.

60      CAESAR.    And you are come in very happy time°
To bear my greeting to the senators,
And tell them that I will not come today.
Cannot, is false; and that I dare not, falser;
I will not come today. Tell them so, Decius.

65      CALPHURNIA.    Say he is sick.

CAESAR.                          Shall Caesar send a lie?
Have I in conquest stretch'd mine arm so far

**66–67** **Have I . . . truth:** Have I made such conquests to be afraid to tell old men the truth?

**75** **stays:** keeps.

**76** **tonight:** last night.

**80** **apply for:** interpret as.

**85–89** **Your statue . . . cognizance:** **Tinctures** are features added to a coat of arms; **relics** are the remains of saints; **cognizance** is a mark identifying one as a lord's follower. Decius interprets Calphurnia's dream as a sign of Caesar's prestige, with great men coming to him to show their political loyalty and reverence.

**96–97** **it were a . . . render'd:** it would be a joke likely to be made.

**102–103** **my dear . . . proceeding:** my very deep desire for your advancement.

**104** **liable:** subservient. Decius says that his love for Caesar forces him to say this, even though he may be overstepping himself.

To be afeard to tell graybeards the truth?°
Decius, go tell them Caesar will not come.

**DECIUS.** Most mighty Caesar, let me know some cause,
70     Lest I be laugh'd at when I tell them so.

**CAESAR.** The cause is in my will, I will not come:
That is enough to satisfy the Senate.
But for your private satisfaction,
Because I love you, I will let you know.
75     Calphurnia here, my wife, stays° me at home:
She dreamt tonight° she saw my statue,
Which, like a fountain with an hundred spouts,
Did run pure blood, and many lusty Romans
Came smiling and did bathe their hands in it.
80     And these does she apply for° warnings and portents
And evils imminent, and on her knee
Hath begg'd that I will stay at home today.

**DECIUS.** This dream is all amiss interpreted,
It was a vision fair and fortunate.
85     Your statue spouting blood in many pipes,
In which so many smiling Romans bath'd,
Signifies that from you great Rome shall suck
Reviving blood, and that great men shall press
For tinctures, stains, relics, and cognizance.°
90     This by Calphurnia's dream is signified.

**CAESAR.** And this way have you well expounded it.

**DECIUS.** I have, when you have heard what I can say;
And know it now: the Senate have concluded
To give this day a crown to mighty Caesar.
95     If you shall send them word you will not come,
Their minds may change. Besides, it were a mock
Apt to be render'd,° for someone to say,
"Break up the Senate till another time,
When Caesar's wife shall meet with better dreams."
100     If Caesar hide himself, shall they not whisper,
"Lo, Caesar is afraid"?
Pardon me, Caesar, for my dear dear love
To your proceeding° bids me tell you this;
And reason to my love is liable.°

105 **CAESAR.** How foolish do your fears seem now, Calphurnia!
I am ashamed I did yield to them.
Give me my robe, for I will go.

112    **your enemy:**  Caesar had recently pardoned Ligarius for his support of Pompey during the civil war.

113    **ague:**  fever.

116    **that revels long a-nights:**  who carouses late into the night.

128–129    **That every . . . upon:**  Brutus grieves to think that not everyone who appears to be a friend is a real friend.

[*Enter* BRUTUS, LIGARIUS, METELLUS CIMBER, CASCA, TREBONIUS, CINNA, *and* PUBLIUS.]

> And look where Publius is come to fetch me.

**PUBLIUS.**   Good morrow, Caesar.

**CAESAR.**                                   Welcome, Publius.
110     What, Brutus, are you stirr'd so early too?
Good morrow, Casca. Caius Ligarius,
Caesar was ne'er so much your enemy°
As that same ague° which hath made you lean.
What is't o'clock?

**BRUTUS.**                     Caesar, 'tis strucken eight.

115   **CAESAR.**   I thank you for your pains and courtesy.

[*Enter* ANTONY.]

> See, Antony, that revels long a-nights,°
> Is notwithstanding up. Good morrow, Antony.

**ANTONY.**   So to most noble Caesar.

**CAESAR.**                                 Bid them prepare within;
I am to blame to be thus waited for.
120     Now, Cinna; now, Metellus; what, Trebonius,
I have an hour's talk in store for you;
Remember that you call on me today;
Be near me, that I may remember you.

**TREBONIUS.**   Caesar, I will [*Aside.*] and so near will I be,
125     That your best friends shall wish I had been further.

**CAESAR.**   Good friends, go in, and taste some wine with me,
And we, like friends, will straightway go together.

**BRUTUS.**   [*Aside.*] That every like is not the same, O Caesar,
The heart of Brutus earns to think upon.°

[*They exit.*]

6–7   **security gives . . . conspiracy:** overconfidence opens the way for enemy plots.

8   **lover:** devoted friend.

10   **suitor:** person presenting a special request to a ruler.

12   **Out of . . . emulation:** beyond the reach of envy.

14   **contrive:** conspire.

4–5   **I would . . . do there:** You could go there and return here before I could explain what you should do there.

6   **constancy:** firmness.

9   **counsel:** a secret.

# SCENE 3. A street near the Capitol. Shortly afterward.

[*Enter* ARTEMIDORUS (*reading a paper*).]

ARTEMIDORUS.    "Caesar, beware of Brutus; take heed of Cassius;
   come not near Casca; have an eye to Cinna; trust not
   Trebonius; mark well Metellus Cimber; Decius Brutus loves
   thee not; thou hast wrong'd Caius Ligarius. There is but
5    one mind in all these men, and it is bent against Caesar. If
   thou beest not immortal, look about you; security gives
   way to conspiracy.° The mighty gods defend thee!
           Thy lover,° Artemidorus."
   Here will I stand till Caesar pass along,
10   And as a suitor° will I give him this.
   My heart laments that virtue cannot live
   Out of the teeth of emulation.°
   If thou read this, O Caesar, thou mayest live;
   If not, the Fates with traitors do contrive.° [*Exit.*]


# SCENE 4. Another Roman street. Immediately after.

[*Enter* PORTIA *and* LUCIUS.]

PORTIA.    I prithee, boy, run to the Senate House;
   Stay not to answer me, but get thee gone.
   Why dost thou stay?

LUCIUS.                    To know my errand, madam.

PORTIA.    I would have had thee there and here again
5    Ere I can tell thee what thou shouldst do there°—
   O constancy,° be strong upon my side;
   Set a huge mountain 'tween my heart and tongue!
   I have a man's mind, but a woman's might.
   How hard it is for women to keep counsel!°—
10   Art thou here yet?

LUCIUS.                    Madam, what should I do?
   Run to the Capitol, and nothing else?
   And so return to you, and nothing else?

PORTIA.    Yes, bring me word, boy, if thy lord look well,
   For he went sickly forth; and take good note
15   What Caesar doth, what suitors press to him.
   Hark, boy, what noise is that?

LUCIUS.    I hear none, madam.

18    **bustling . . . fray:** noise of some activity such as a fight.

20    **Sooth:** truly.

37    **void:** empty.

42–43    **Brutus hath . . . grant:** Portia makes up this excuse about Brutus's petition to explain her nervousness to Lucius.

44    **commend me to my lord:** send my regards to my husband.

**PORTIA.**                                   Prithee, listen well.
  I heard a bustling rumor, like a fray,°
  And the wind brings it from the Capitol.

20  **LUCIUS.**   Sooth,° madam, I hear nothing.

[*Enter the* SOOTHSAYER.]

**PORTIA.**   Come hither, fellow; which way hast thou been?

**SOOTHSAYER.**   At mine own house, good lady.

**PORTIA.**   What is't a'clock?

**SOOTHSAYER.**                                   About the ninth hour, lady.

**PORTIA.**   Is Caesar yet gone to the Capitol?

25  **SOOTHSAYER.**   Madam, not yet; I go to take my stand,
  To see him pass on to the Capitol.

**PORTIA.**   Thou hast some suit to Caesar, hast thou not?

**SOOTHSAYER.**   That I have, lady, if it will please Caesar
  To be so good to Caesar as to hear me:
30    I shall beseech him to befriend himself.

**PORTIA.**   Why, know'st thou any harm's intended towards him?

**SOOTHSAYER.**   None that I know will be, much that I fear may
    chance.
  Good morrow to you. Here the street is narrow;
  The throng that follows Caesar at the heels,
35  Of senators, of praetors, common suitors,
  Will crowd a feeble man almost to death.
  I'll get me to a place more void,° and there
  Speak to great Caesar as he comes along.

[*Exit.*]

**PORTIA.**   I must go in. Ay me! How weak a thing
40  The heart of woman is! O Brutus,
  The heavens speed thee in thine enterprise!
  Sure, the boy heard me—Brutus hath a suit
  That Caesar will not grant.°—O, I grow faint.—
  Run, Lucius, and commend me to my lord,°
45  Say I am merry. Come to me again,
  And bring me word what he doth say to thee.

[*They exit separately.*]

3    **schedule:** document.

10    **Sirrah:** an insulting form of address to an inferior.

# Act 3

## SCENE 1. The Capitol in Rome. The ides of March.

[*Flourish. Enter* CAESAR, BRUTUS, CASSIUS, CASCA, DECIUS, METELLUS, TREBONIUS, CINNA, ANTONY, PUBLIUS, POPILIUS, LEPIDUS, ARTEMIDORUS, *and the* SOOTHSAYER.]

**CAESAR.**   The ides of March are come.

**SOOTHSAYER.**   Ay, Caesar, but not gone.

**ARTEMIDORUS.**   Hail, Caesar! Read this schedule.°

**DECIUS.**   Trebonius doth desire you to o'er-read,
5      (At your best leisure) this his humble suit.

**ARTEMIDORUS.**   O Caesar, read mine first; for mine's a suit
      That touches Caesar nearer. Read it, great Caesar.

**CAESAR.**   What touches us ourself shall be last serv'd.

**ARTEMIDORUS.**   Delay not, Caesar, read it instantly.

10   **CAESAR.**   What, is the fellow mad?

**PUBLIUS.**                          Sirrah,° give place.

**CASSIUS.**   What, urge you your petitions in the street?
      Come to the Capitol.

[CAESAR *enters the Capitol, the rest following.*]

**POPILIUS.**   I wish your enterprise today may thrive.

**CASSIUS.**   What enterprise, Popilius?

**POPILIUS.**                          Fare you well. [*Leaves him and
      joins* CAESAR.]

15   **BRUTUS.**   What said Popilius Lena?

**CASSIUS.**   He wish'd today our enterprise might thrive.

18    **makes:** makes his way.

19    **be sudden ... prevention:** be quick, for we fear that we will be stopped.

21    **turn back:** return alive.
22    **constant:** resolute.

28    **presently prefer:** immediately present.

29    **address'd:** ready.

33    **puissant:** powerful.

36–43    **These couchings ... fawning:** This kneeling and humble behavior might influence ordinary men and turn laws and decisions that have been firmly es-
tablished into the whims of children. But don't be foolish enough to think
that Caesar's emotions are so out of control that he will be swayed from the
proper course with compliments, bowing, and fawning like a dog.

46    **spurn thee ... cur:** kick you like a dog.

47–48    **Know ... satisfied:** Caesar is not unjust, nor will he grant a pardon without
good reason.

I fear our purpose is discovered.

**BRUTUS.**   Look how he makes° to Caesar; mark him.

**CASSIUS.**   Casca, be sudden, for we fear prevention.°
20   Brutus, what shall be done? If this be known,
Cassius or Caesar never shall turn back,°
For I will slay myself.

**BRUTUS.**                    Cassius, be constant;°
Popilius Lena speaks not of our purposes,
For look he smiles, and Caesar doth not change.

25   **CASSIUS.**   Trebonius knows his time; for look you, Brutus,
He draws Mark Antony out of the way.

[*ANTONY and TREBONIUS exit.*]

**DECIUS.**   Where is Metellus Cimber? Let him go
And presently prefer° his suit to Caesar.

**BRUTUS.**   He is address'd;° press near and second him.

30   **CINNA.**   Casca, you are the first that rears your hand.

**CAESAR.**   Are we all ready? What is now amiss
That Caesar and his Senate must redress?

**METELLUS.**   Most high, most mighty, and most puissant° Caesar,
Metellus Cimber throws before thy seat
35   An humble heart. [*Kneeling.*]

**CAESAR.**                    I must prevent thee, Cimber.
These couchings and these lowly courtesies
Might fire the blood of ordinary men,
And turn preordinance and first decree
Into the [law] of children. Be not fond
40   To think that Caesar bears such rebel blood
That will be thaw'd from the true quality
With that which melteth fools—I mean sweet words,
Low-crooked curtsies, and base spaniel fawning.°
Thy brother by decree is banished;
45   If thou dost bend, and pray, and fawn for him,
I spurn thee like a cur° out of my way.
Know, Caesar doth not wrong, nor without cause
Will he be satisfied.°

**METELLUS.**   Is there no voice more worthy than my own,
50   To sound more sweetly in great Caesar's ear
For the repealing of my banish'd brother?

54    **freedom of repeal:**  permission to be recalled from exile.

57    **enfranchisement:**  restoration of his rights as a citizen.

62    **no fellow in the firmament:**  no equal in the heavens. (Because the North Star appears directly above the North Pole, it seems to be stationary; the other stars seem to change position as the earth rotates.)

67    **apprehensive:**  capable of reason.

72    **constant:**  determined.

74    **lift up Olympus:**  try to do the impossible. (Olympus is a mountain in Greece; in classical mythology, it was the home of the gods.)

75    **bootless:**  in vain.

77    ***Et tu, Brute?:***  Latin for, "And you, Brutus?" (He is shocked that even Brutus would betray him.)

80    **pulpits:**  platforms for public speaking.

83    **ambition's debt is paid:**  Ambition received what was due to it.

**BRUTUS.**   I kiss thy hand, but not in flattery, Caesar;
Desiring thee that Publius Cimber may
Have an immediate freedom of repeal.°

55  **CAESAR.**   What, Brutus?

**CASSIUS.**                  Pardon, Caesar! Caesar, pardon!
As low as to thy foot doth Cassius fall,
To beg enfranchisement° for Publius Cimber.

**CAESAR.**   I could be well mov'd, if I were as you;
If I could pray to move, prayers would move me;
60  But I am constant as the northern star,
Of whose true-fix'd and resting quality
There is no fellow in the firmament.°
The skies are painted with unnumb'red sparks,
They are all fire and every one doth shine;
65  But there's but one in all doth hold his place.
So in the world: 'tis furnish'd well with men,
And men are flesh and blood, and apprehensive;°
Yet in the number I do know but one
That unassailable holds on his rank,
70  Unshak'd of motion; and that I am he,
Let me a little show it, even in this—
That I was constant° Cimber should be banish'd,
And constant do remain to keep him so.

**CINNA.**   O Caesar—

**CAESAR.**                  Hence! Wilt thou lift up Olympus?°

75  **DECIUS.**   Great Caesar—

**CAESAR.**                  Doth not Brutus bootless° kneel?

**CASCA.**   Speak hands for me!

[*They stab* CAESAR.]

**CAESAR.**   *Et tu, Brute?*°—Then fall Caesar. [*Dies.*]

**CINNA.**   Liberty! Freedom! Tyranny is dead!
Run hence, proclaim, cry it about the streets.

80  **CASSIUS.**   Some to the common pulpits,° and cry out
"Liberty, freedom, and enfranchisement!"

**BRUTUS.**   People, and senators, be not affrighted.
Fly not; stand still; ambition's debt is paid.°

86    **confounded with this mutiny:** confused by this uproar.


94    **abide:** pay the penalty for.


96    **amaz'd:** stunned.

98    **As:** as if.
98    **Fates:** in classical mythology, three goddesses who determined human destiny.

99–100    **'tis but . . . upon:** It is only the time of death and prolonging of life that men care about.


114   **in sport:** for entertainment. (These prophecies—of reenacting Caesar's assassination in countries not yet founded and in languages not yet known—are fulfilled by the performance of Shakespeare's play.)
115   **Pompey's basis:** the base of Pompey's statue.

**CASCA.**   Go to the pulpit, Brutus.

**DECIUS.**                                    And Cassius too.

85   **BRUTUS.**   Where's Publius?

**CINNA.**   Here, quite confounded with this mutiny.°

**METELLUS.**   Stand fast together, lest some friend of Caesar's
Should chance—

**BRUTUS.**   Talk not of standing. Publius, good cheer,
90   There is no harm intended to your person,
Nor to no Roman else. So tell them, Publius.

**CASSIUS.**   And leave us, Publius, lest that the people,
Rushing on us should do your age some mischief.

**BRUTUS.**   Do so; and let no man abide° this deed,
95   But we the doers.

[*All but the* CONSPIRATORS *exit. Enter* TREBONIUS.]

**CASSIUS.**   Where is Antony?

**TREBONIUS.**                             Fled to his house amaz'd.°
Men, wives, and children stare, cry out and run,
As° it were doomsday.

**BRUTUS.**                          Fates,° we will know your pleasures.
That we shall die, we know, 'tis but the time,
100   And drawing days out, that men stand upon.°

**CASCA.**   Why, he that cuts off twenty years of life
Cuts off so many years of fearing death.

**BRUTUS.**   Grant that, and then is death a benefit.
So are we Caesar's friends, that have abridg'd
105   His time of fearing death. Stoop, Romans, stoop,
And let us bathe our hands in Caesar's blood
Up to the elbows, and besmear our swords.
Then walk we forth, even to the marketplace,
And waving our red weapons o'er our heads,
110   Let's all cry "Peace, freedom, and liberty!"

**CASSIUS.**   Stoop then, and wash. How many ages hence
Shall this our lofty scene be acted over
In states unborn and accents yet unknown!

**BRUTUS.**   How many times shall Caesar bleed in sport,°
115   That now on Pompey's basis° [lies] along
No worthier than the dust!

126 **honest:** honorable.

130 **vouchsafe:** allow.
131 **be resolv'd:** receive a satisfactory explanation.

136 **Thorough . . . state:** through all the dangers of this new and uncertain state of affairs.

142 **presently:** immediately.
143 **well to friend:** as a good friend.

145–146 **my misgiving . . . purpose:** My suspicions always turn out to be close to the truth.

**CASSIUS.**                    So oft as that shall be,
   So often shall the knot of us be call'd
   The men that gave their country liberty.

**DECIUS.**    What, shall we forth?

**CASSIUS.**                        Ay, every man away.
120   Brutus shall lead, and we will grace his heels
   With the most boldest and best hearts of Rome.

[*Enter a* SERVANT.]

**BRUTUS.**    Soft, who comes here? A friend of Antony's.

**SERVANT.**    Thus, Brutus, did my master bid me kneel;
   Thus did Mark Antony bid me fall down;
125   And, being prostrate, thus he bade me say;
   Brutus is noble, wise, valiant, and honest;°
   Caesar was mighty, bold, royal, and loving.
   Say, I love Brutus, and I honor him;
   Say, I fear'd Caesar, honor'd him, and lov'd him.
130   If Brutus will vouchsafe° that Antony
   May safely come to him, and be resolv'd°
   How Caesar hath deserv'd to lie in death,
   Mark Antony shall not love Caesar dead
   So well as Brutus living; but will follow
135   The fortunes and affairs of noble Brutus
   Thorough the hazards of this untrod state°
   With all true faith. So says my master Antony.

**BRUTUS.**    Thy master is a wise and valiant Roman;
   I never thought him worse.
140   Tell him, so please him come unto this place,
   He shall be satisfied and, by my honor,
   Depart untouch'd.

**SERVANT.**                I'll fetch him presently.° [*Exit* SERVANT.]

**BRUTUS.**    I know that we shall have him well to friend.°

**CASSIUS.**    I wish we may; but yet have I a mind
145   That fears him much; and my misgiving still
   Falls shrewdly to the purpose.°

[*Enter* ANTONY.]

**BRUTUS.**    But here comes Antony. Welcome, Mark Antony.

**ANTONY.**    O mighty Caesar! dost thou lie so low?
   Are all thy conquests, glories, triumphs, spoils,

152    **let blood:** killed. **rank:** swollen with disease. In Antony's metaphor, political corruption is like a disease that must be treated by drawing blood from the patient.

157    **bear me hard:** have a grudge against me.
158    **purpled:** blood-stained.

160    **apt:** ready.
161    **mean of death:** way of dying.

169    **pitiful:** full of pity.

170–172    **And pity . . . Caesar:** Brutus says that just as one fire can extinguish another, their pity for Rome overcame their pity for Caesar.
173    **leaden:** blunt.
174    **Our arms . . . malice:** our arms seemingly full of malice (because still blood-stained).

177–178    **Your voice . . . dignities:** You will have equal say in deciding who will hold political office.

181    **deliver you the cause:** explain.

| 150 | Shrunk to this little measure? Fare thee well. |
| | I know not, gentlemen, what you intend, |
| | Who else must be let blood,° who else is rank.° |
| | If I myself, there is no hour so fit |
| | As Caesar's death's hour, nor no instrument |
| 155 | Of half that worth as those your swords, made rich |
| | With the most noble blood of all this world. |
| | I do beseech ye, if you bear me hard,° |
| | Now, whilst your purpled° hands do reek and smoke, |
| | Fulfill your pleasure. Live a thousand years, |
| 160 | I shall not find myself so apt° to die; |
| | No place will please me so, no mean of death,° |
| | As here by Caesar, and by you cut off, |
| | The choice and master spirits of this age. |

**BRUTUS.**  O Antony! beg not your death of us.
150     Though now we must appear bloody and cruel,

165   Though now we must appear bloody and cruel,
    As by our hands and this our present act
    You see we do, yet see you but our hands
    And this the bleeding business they have done.
    Our hearts you see not, they are pitiful;°
170   And pity to the general wrong of Rome—
    As fire drives out fire, so pity pity—
    Hath done this deed on Caesar.° For your part,
    To you our swords have leaden° points, Mark Antony;
    Our arms in strength of malice,° and our hearts
175   Of brothers' temper, do receive you in
    With all kind love, good thoughts, and reverence.

**CASSIUS.**  Your voice shall be as strong as any man's
    In the disposing of new dignities.°

**BRUTUS.**  Only be patient till we have appeas'd
180   The multitude, beside themselves with fear,
    And then we will deliver you the cause°
    Why I, that did love Caesar when I struck him,
    Have thus proceeded.

**ANTONY.**            I doubt not of your wisdom.
    Let each man render me his bloody hand.
185   First, Marcus Brutus, will I shake with you;
    Next, Caius Cassius, do I take your hand;
    Now, Decius Brutus, yours; now yours, Metellus;
    Yours, Cinna; and, my valiant Casca, yours;

191    **credit:**  reputation (because he was Caesar's friend).

192    **conceit:**  judge, consider.

199    **corse:**  corpse.

202    **close:**  come to an agreement.

204    **bay'd:**  cornered like a hunted animal.  **hart:**  male deer. Antony plays on the words *hart* and *heart* later in this speech.

206    **Sign'd in thy spoil:**  marked with your slaughter.  **lethe:**  bloodstream. (In classical mythology, Lethe was a river in Hades, the underworld.)

213    **modesty:**  restraint.

216    **prick'd:**  marked down; counted.

217    **on:**  proceed.

222    **wherein:**  in what way.

224    **good regard:**  sound considerations.

Though last, not least in love, yours, good Trebonius.
190 Gentlemen all—alas, what shall I say?
My credit° now stands on such slippery ground
That one of two bad ways you must conceit° me,
Either a coward or a flatterer.
That I did love thee, Caesar, O, 'tis true;
195 If then thy spirit look upon us now,
Shall it not grieve thee dearer than thy death,
To see thy Antony making his peace,
Shaking the bloody fingers of thy foes,
Most noble, in the presence of thy corse?°
200 Had I as many eyes as thou hast wounds,
Weeping as fast as they stream forth thy blood,
It would become me better than to close°
In terms of friendship with thine enemies.
Pardon me, Julius! Here wast thou bay'd,° brave hart,°
205 Here didst thou fall, and here thy hunters stand,
Sign'd in thy spoil,° and crimson'd in thy lethe.°
O world! thou wast the forest to this hart,
And this indeed, O world, the heart of thee.
How like a deer, strooken by many princes,
210 Dost thou here lie!

CASSIUS.     Mark Antony—

ANTONY.                          Pardon me, Caius Cassius!
The enemies of Caesar shall say this:
Then, in a friend, it is cold modesty.°

CASSIUS.     I blame you not for praising Caesar so,
215 But what compact mean you to have with us?
Will you be prick'd° in number of our friends,
Or shall we on,° and not depend on you?

ANTONY.     Therefore I took your hands, but was indeed
Sway'd from the point by looking down on Caesar.
220 Friends am I with you all, and love you all,
Upon this hope, that you shall give me reasons
Why, and wherein,° Caesar was dangerous.

BRUTUS.     Or else were this a savage spectacle.
Our reasons are so full of good regard°
225 That were you, Antony, the son of Caesar,
You should be satisfied.

ANTONY.                          That's all I seek;

227 **am moreover suitor:** Furthermore I ask.
228 **Produce:** bring forth.

230 **order:** ceremony.

238 **protest:** declare.

242 **advantage:** benefit.
243 **fall:** happen.

257 **the tide of times:** all of history.

And am moreover suitor° that I may
Produce° his body to the marketplace,
And in the pulpit, as becomes a friend,
230    Speak in the order° of his funeral.

**BRUTUS.**    You shall, Mark Antony.

**CASSIUS.**                    Brutus, a word with you.
[*Aside to* BRUTUS.] You know not what you do. Do not consent
That Antony speak in his funeral.
Know you how much the people may be mov'd
235    By that which he will utter?

**BRUTUS.**                By your pardon—
I will myself into the pulpit first,
And show the reason of our Caesar's death.
What Antony shall speak, I will protest°
He speaks by leave and by permission;
240    And that we are contented Caesar shall
Have all true rites and lawful ceremonies.
It shall advantage° more than do us wrong.

**CASSIUS.**    I know not what may fall,° I like it not.

**BRUTUS.**    Mark Antony, here, take you Caesar's body.
245    You shall not in your funeral speech blame us,
But speak all good you can devise of Caesar,
And say you do't by our permission;
Else shall you not have any hand at all
About his funeral. And you shall speak
250    In the same pulpit whereto I am going,
After my speech is ended.

**ANTONY.**               Be it so;
I do desire no more.

**BRUTUS.**    Prepare the body then, and follow us.

[*They exit.* ANTONY *remains.*]

**ANTONY.**    O pardon me, thou bleeding piece of earth,
255    That I am meek and gentle with these butchers!
Thou art the ruins of the noblest man
That ever lived in the tide of times.°
Woe to the hand that shed this costly blood!
Over thy wounds now do I prophesy
260    (Which like dumb mouths do ope their ruby lips
To beg the voice and utterance of my tongue)

262    **light:** fall.

264    **cumber:** burden; harass.

265    **in use:** common.

268    **quartered:** cut to pieces.

269    **custom of fell deeds:** familiarity with cruel deeds.

270    **ranging:** roving (like an animal in search of prey).

271    **Ate:** goddess of vengeance and strife.

273    **Havoc:** a battle cry to kill without mercy. (Only a king could give this order.)

275    **carrion:** dead and rotting.

282    **big:** swollen with grief.

286    **seven leagues:** twenty-one miles.

287    **Post:** Ride back quickly.

290    **Hie hence:** Go quickly from here.

292    **try:** test.

294    **cruel issue:** outcome of cruelty.

A curse shall light° upon the limbs of men;
Domestic fury and fierce civil strife
Shall cumber° all the parts of Italy;
265  Blood and destruction shall be so in use,°
And dreadful objects so familiar,
That mothers shall but smile when they behold
Their infants quartered° with the hands of war;
All pity chok'd with custom of fell deeds;°
270  And Caesar's spirit, ranging° for revenge,
With Ate° by his side come hot from hell,
Shall in these confines with a monarch's voice
Cry "Havoc!"° and let slip the dogs of war,
That this foul deed shall smell above the earth
275  With carrion° men, groaning for burial.

[*Enter* OCTAVIUS's SERVANT.]

You serve Octavius Caesar, do you not?

**SERVANT.**   I do, Mark Antony.

**ANTONY.**   Caesar did write for him to come to Rome.

**SERVANT.**   He did receive his letters and is coming,
280  And bid me say to you by word of mouth—
[*Seeing the body.*] O Caesar!—

**ANTONY.**   Thy heart is big;° get thee apart and weep.
Passion, I see, is catching, [for] mine eyes,
Seeing those beads of sorrow stand in thine,
285  Began to water. Is thy master coming?

**SERVANT.**   He lies tonight within seven leagues° of Rome.

**ANTONY.**   Post° back with speed, and tell him what hath chanc'd.
Here is a mourning Rome, a dangerous Rome,
No Rome of safety for Octavius yet;
290  Hie hence,° and tell him so. Yet stay awhile,
Thou shalt not back till I have borne this corse
Into the marketplace. There shall I try,°
In my oration, how the people take
The cruel issue° of these bloody men,
295  According to the which thou shalt discourse
To young Octavius of the state of things.
Lend me your hand.

[*They exit (with* CAESAR's *body*).]

1 **satisfied:** The common people (**plebeians**) demand a full explanation of the assassination.

4 **part the numbers:** divide the crowd.

7 **rendered:** presented.

10 **severally:** separately.

12 **last:** end of the speech.
13 **lovers:** dear friends.

15 **have respect . . . honor:** remember that I am honorable.
16 **Censure:** judge.
17 **senses:** understanding.

28 **bondman:** slave.
29 **rude:** uncivilized.

**SCENE 2. The Roman Forum, the city's great public square. A few days later.**

[*Enter* BRUTUS *and* CASSIUS *with the* PLEBEIANS.]

**PLEBEIANS.**   We will be satisfied!° Let us be satisfied!

**BRUTUS.**   Then follow me, and give me audience, friends.
Cassius, go you into the other street,
And part the numbers.°
5   Those that will hear me speak, let 'em stay here;
Those that will follow Cassius, go with him;
And public reasons shall be rendered°
Of Caesar's death.

**FIRST PLEBEIAN.**   I will hear Brutus speak.

**SECOND PLEBEIAN.**   I will hear Cassius, and compare their reasons,
10   When severally° we hear them rendered.

[*Exit* CASSIUS *with some of the* PLEBEIANS. BRUTUS *goes into the pulpit.*]

**THIRD PLEBEIAN.**   The noble Brutus is ascended; silence!

**BRUTUS.**   Be patient till the last.°
Romans, countrymen, and lovers,° hear me for my cause,
and be silent, that you may hear. Believe me for mine
15   honor, and have respect to mine honor,° that you may
believe. Censure° me in your wisdom, and awake your
senses,° that you may the better judge. If there be any in
this assembly, any dear friend of Caesar's, to him I say, that
Brutus' love to Caesar was no less than his. If then that
20   friend demand why Brutus rose against Caesar, this is my
answer; Not that I lov'd Caesar less, but that I lov'd Rome
more. Had you rather Caesar were living, and die all slaves,
than that Caesar were dead, to live all free men? As Caesar
lov'd me, I weep for him; as he was fortunate, I rejoice at it;
25   as he was valiant, I honor him; but, as he was ambitious, I
slew him. There is tears for his love; joy for his fortune;
honor for his valor; and death for his ambition. Who is
here so base that would be a bondman?° If any, speak, for
him have I offended. Who is here so rude,° that would not
30   be a Roman? If any, speak, for him have I offended. Who
is here so vile that will not love his country? If any, speak,
for him have I offended. I pause for a reply.

**ALL.**   None, Brutus, none.

| 35–36 | **The question . . . Capitol:** The reasons for his death are recorded in the public archives of the Capitol. |
| 37 | **extenuated:** diminished. |
| 38 | **enforc'd:** exaggerated. |

| 41 | **a place in the commonwealth:** citizenship in a free republic. |

| 48 | **parts:** qualities. |

| 55–56 | **Do grace . . . glories:** Pay respect to Caesar's body and listen respectfully to Antony's speech dealing with Caesar's glories. |

| 61 | **public chair:** pulpit. |

| 63 | **beholding:** indebted. |

**BRUTUS.**    Then none have I offended. I have done no more to
35    Caesar than you shall do to Brutus. The question of his
death is enroll'd in the Capitol;° his glory not
extenuated,° wherein he was worthy; nor his offenses
enforc'd,° for which he suffer'd death.

[*Enter* MARK ANTONY (*and others*) *with* CAESAR's *body.*]

Here comes his body, mourn'd by Mark Antony, who, though
40    he had no hand in his death, shall receive the benefit of his
dying, a place in the commonwealth,° as which of you shall
not? With this I depart, that, as I slew my best lover for the
good of Rome, I have the same dagger for myself, when it
shall please my country to need my death.

45    **ALL.**    Live, Brutus, live, live!

**FIRST PLEBEIAN.**    Bring him with triumph home unto his house.

**SECOND PLEBEIAN.**    Give him a statue with his ancestors.

**THIRD PLEBEIAN.**    Let him be Caesar.

**FOURTH PLEBEIAN.**                      Caesar's better parts°
Shall be crown'd in Brutus.

**FIRST PLEBEIAN.**                      We'll bring him to his house
50    With shouts and clamors.

**BRUTUS.**                      My countrymen—

**SECOND PLEBEIAN.**    Peace, silence! Brutus speaks.

**FIRST PLEBEIAN.**    Peace, ho!

**BRUTUS.**    Good countrymen, let me depart alone,
And, for my sake, stay here with Antony.
55    Do grace to Caesar's corpse, and grace his speech
Tending to Caesar's glories,° which Mark Antony
(By our permission) is allow'd to make.
I do entreat you, not a man depart,
Save I alone, till Antony have spoke.

60    **FIRST PLEBEIAN.**    Stay, ho, and let us hear Mark Antony.

**THIRD PLEBEIAN.**    Let him go up into the public chair;°
We'll hear him. Noble Antony, go up.

**ANTONY.**    For Brutus' sake, I am beholding° to you.

[*Goes into the pulpit.*]

**FOURTH PLEBEIAN.**    What does he say of Brutus?

74   **interred:** buried.


78   **answer'd:** paid the penalty for.
79   **leave:** permission.


87   **general coffers:** public treasury.


93   **Lupercal:** See act 1, scene 1, line 67.

95   **Which he . . . refuse:** the incident described by Casca in act 1, scene 2, lines
     234–242.

**THIRD PLEBEIAN.**                                    He says, for Brutus' sake,
65     He finds himself beholding to us all.

    **FOURTH PLEBEIAN.**     'Twere best he speak no harm of Brutus here!

    **FIRST PLEBEIAN.**     This Caesar was a tyrant.

    **THIRD PLEBEIAN.**                                    Nay, that's certain.
    We are blest that Rome is rid of him.

    **SECOND PLEBEIAN.**     Peace, let us hear what Antony can say.

70     **ANTONY.**     You gentle Romans—

[*The noise continues.*]

    **ALL.**                                    Peace, ho, let us hear him.

    **ANTONY.**     Friends, Romans, countrymen, lend me your ears!
    I come to bury Caesar, not to praise him.
    The evil that men do lives after them,
    The good is oft interred° with their bones;
75     So let it be with Caesar. The noble Brutus
    Hath told you Caesar was ambitious;
    If it were so, it was a grievous fault,
    And grievously hath Caesar answer'd° it.
    Here, under leave° of Brutus and the rest
80     (For Brutus is an honorable man,
    So are they all, all honorable men),
    Come I to speak in Caesar's funeral.
    He was my friend, faithful and just to me;
    But Brutus says he was ambitious,
85     And Brutus is an honorable man.
    He hath brought many captives home to Rome,
    Whose ransoms did the general coffers° fill;
    Did this in Caesar seem ambitious?
    When that the poor have cried, Caesar hath wept;
90     Ambition should be made of sterner stuff:
    Yet Brutus says he was ambitious;
    And Brutus is an honorable man.
    You all did see that on the Lupercal°
    I thrice presented him a kingly crown,
95     Which he did thrice refuse.° Was this ambition?
    Yet Brutus says he was ambitious;
    And sure he is an honorable man.
    I speak not to disprove what Brutus spoke,
    But here I am to speak what I do know.

110    **Mark'd ye:** Did you listen to?

112    **dear abide it:** pay dearly for it.

118    **none . . . reverence:** No one is humble enough to honor him.

128    **commons:** common people.

131    **napkins:** handkerchiefs. (Antony refers to the custom of dipping cloths in the blood of martyrs.)

135    **issue:** children.

| | |
|---|---|
| 100 | You all did love him once, not without cause; |
| | What cause withholds you then to mourn for him? |
| | O judgment, thou art fled to brutish beasts, |
| | And men have lost their reason. Bear with me, |
| | My heart is in the coffin there with Caesar, |
| 105 | And I must pause till it come back to me. |

FIRST PLEBEIAN.   Methinks there is much reason in his sayings.

SECOND PLEBEIAN.   If thou consider rightly of the matter,
Caesar has had great wrong.

THIRD PLEBEIAN.                    Has he, masters?
I fear there will a worse come in his place.

110   FOURTH PLEBEIAN.   Mark'd ye° his words? He would not take
the crown,
Therefore, 'tis certain he was not ambitious.

FIRST PLEBEIAN.   If it be found so, some will dear abide it.°

SECOND PLEBEIAN.   Poor soul, his eyes are red as fire with weeping.

THIRD PLEBEIAN.   There's not a nobler man in Rome than Antony.

115   FOURTH PLEBEIAN.   Now mark him, he begins again to speak.

| | |
|---|---|
| | ANTONY.   But yesterday the word of Caesar might |
| | Have stood against the world; now lies he there, |
| | And none so poor to do him reverence.° |
| | O masters! if I were dispos'd to stir |
| 120 | Your hearts and minds to mutiny and rage, |
| | I should do Brutus wrong and Cassius wrong, |
| | Who (you all know) are honorable men. |
| | I will not do them wrong; I rather choose |
| | To wrong the dead, to wrong myself and you, |
| 125 | Than I will wrong such honorable men. |
| | But here's a parchment with the seal of Caesar; |
| | I found it in his closet, 'tis his will. |
| | Let but the commons° hear this testament— |
| | Which, pardon me, I do not mean to read— |
| 130 | And they would go and kiss dead Caesar's wounds, |
| | And dip their napkins° in his sacred blood; |
| | Yea, beg a hair of him for memory, |
| | And dying, mention it within their wills, |
| | Bequeathing it as a rich legacy |
| 135 | Unto their issue.° |

139   **meet:**  proper.

148   **o'ershot myself:**  gone further than I intended.

164   **far:**  farther.

167   **mantle:**  cloak; toga.

**FOURTH PLEBEIAN.**   We'll hear the will; read it, Mark Antony.

**ALL.**   The will, the will! we will hear Caesar's will!

**ANTONY.**   Have patience, gentle friends, I must not read it.
It is not meet° you know how Caesar lov'd you:
140     You are not wood, you are not stones, but men;
And being men, hearing the will of Caesar,
It will inflame you, it will make you mad.
'Tis good you know not that you are his heirs,
For if you should, O, what would come of it?

145 **FOURTH PLEBEIAN.**   Read the will, we'll hear it, Antony.
You shall read us the will, Caesar's will.

**ANTONY.**   Will you be patient? Will you stay awhile?
I have o'ershot myself° to tell you of it.
I fear I wrong the honorable men
150     Whose daggers have stabb'd Caesar; I do fear it.

**FOURTH PLEBEIAN.**   They were traitors; honorable men!

**ALL.**   The will! the testament!

**SECOND PLEBEIAN.**   They were villains, murderers. The will,
read the will!

**ANTONY.**   You will compel me then to read the will?
155     Then make a ring about the corpse of Caesar,
And let me show you him that made the will.
Shall I descend? And will you give me leave?

**ALL.**   Come down.

**SECOND PLEBEIAN.**   Descend.

160 **THIRD PLEBEIAN.**   You shall have leave.

[*ANTONY comes down from the pulpit.*]

**FOURTH PLEBEIAN.**   A ring, stand round.

**FIRST PLEBEIAN.**   Stand from the hearse, stand from the body.

**SECOND PLEBEIAN.**   Room for Antony, most noble Antony.

**ANTONY.**   Nay, press not so upon me; stand far° off.

165 **ALL.**   Stand back; room, bear back.

**ANTONY.**   If you have tears, prepare to shed them now.
You all do know this mantle.° I remember
The first time ever Caesar put it on;
'Twas on a summer's evening, in his tent,

170    **Nervii:** a fierce Gallic tribe defeated by Caesar in 57 B.C.

172    **rent:** rip.

176–177    **As rushing . . . no:** as if rushing outside to learn for certain whether or not Brutus so cruelly and unnaturally "knocked."

178    **angel:** favorite.

189    **flourish'd:** swaggered.

191    **dint:** impression.

192–194    **Kind souls . . . traitors:** In a dramatic gesture, Antony uncovers Caesar's mutilated body after remarking how much the commoners weep when they gaze merely upon Caesar's mutilated clothing.

| 170 | That day he overcame the Nervii.° |
| | Look, in this place ran Cassius' dagger through; |
| | See what a rent° the envious Casca made; |
| | Through this the well-beloved Brutus stabb'd, |
| | And as he pluck'd his cursed steel away, |
| 175 | Mark how the blood of Caesar followed it, |
| | As rushing out of doors, to be resolv'd |
| | If Brutus so unkindly knock'd or no;° |
| | For Brutus, as you know, was Caesar's angel.° |
| | Judge, O you gods, how dearly Caesar lov'd him! |
| 180 | This was the most unkindest cut of all; |
| | For when the noble Caesar saw him stab, |
| | Ingratitude, more strong than traitors' arms, |
| | Quite vanquish'd him. Then burst his mighty heart, |
| | And, in his mantle muffling up his face, |
| 185 | Even at the base of Pompey's statue |
| | (Which all the while ran blood) great Caesar fell. |
| | O, what a fall was there, my countrymen! |
| | Then I, and you, and all of us fell down, |
| | Whilst bloody treason flourish'd° over us. |
| 190 | O now you weep, and I perceive you feel |
| | The dint° of pity. These are gracious drops. |
| | Kind souls, what weep you when you but behold |
| | Our Caesar's vesture wounded? Look you here, [*Lifting* |
| | CAESAR's *mantle.*] |
| | Here is himself, marr'd as you see with traitors.° |

| 195 | FIRST PLEBEIAN.   O piteous spectacle! |

SECOND PLEBEIAN.   O noble Caesar!

THIRD PLEBEIAN.   O woeful day!

FOURTH PLEBEIAN.   O traitors, villains!

FIRST PLEBEIAN.   O most bloody sight!

| 200 | SECOND PLEBEIAN.   We will be reveng'd. |

ALL.   Revenge! About! Seek! Burn! Fire! Kill! Slay!
Let not a traitor live!

ANTONY.   Stay, countrymen.

FIRST PLEBEIAN.   Peace there, hear the noble Antony.

| 205 | SECOND PLEBEIAN.   We'll hear him, we'll follow him, we'll die |
| | with him. |

209     **private griefs:** personal grievances. Antony suggests that the conspirators killed Caesar not for the public reasons Brutus has declared but rather for personal, and therefore less worthy, motives.

217–219     **For I have . . . blood:** Antony claims that he doesn't have the cleverness (**wit**), fluency (**words**), high personal standing or reputation (**worth**), gestures (**action**), and manner of speaking (**utterance**) of a skilled orator.

219     **right on:** straightforwardly.

224     **ruffle up:** enrage.

238     **several:** individual. **drachmas:** silver coins.

240     **royal:** most generous.

**ANTONY.** Good friends, sweet friends, let me not stir you up
To such a sudden flood of mutiny.
They that have done this deed are honorable.
What private griefs° they have, alas, I know not,
210     That made them do it. They are wise and honorable,
And will, no doubt, with reasons answer you.
I come not, friends, to steal away your hearts.
I am no orator, as Brutus is;
But (as you know me all) a plain blunt man
215     That love my friend, and that they know full well
That gave me public leave to speak of him.
For I have neither wit, nor words, nor worth,
Action, nor utterance, nor the power of speech
To stir men's blood;° I only speak right on.°
220     I tell you that which you yourselves do know,
Show you sweet Caesar's wounds, poor, poor, dumb mouths,
And bid them speak for me. But were I Brutus,
And Brutus Antony, there were an Antony
Would ruffle up° your spirits, and put a tongue
225     In every wound of Caesar, that should move
The stones of Rome to rise and mutiny.

**ALL.** We'll mutiny.

**FIRST PLEBEIAN.** We'll burn the house of Brutus.

**THIRD PLEBEIAN.** Away then, come, seek the conspirators.

**ANTONY.** Yet hear me, countrymen, yet hear me speak.

230  **ALL.** Peace, ho, hear Antony, most noble Antony!

**ANTONY.** Why, friends, you go to do you know not what.
Wherein hath Caesar thus deserv'd your loves?
Alas, you know not! I must tell you then;
You have forgot the will I told you of.

235  **ALL.** Most true. The will! Let's stay and hear the will.

**ANTONY.** Here is the will, and under Caesar's seal:
To every Roman citizen he gives,
To every several° man, seventy-five drachmas.°

**SECOND PLEBEIAN.** Most noble Caesar! we'll revenge his death!

240  **THIRD PLEBEIAN.** O royal° Caesar!

**ANTONY.** Hear me with patience.

**ALL.** Peace, ho!

244 **orchards:** gardens.

246 **common pleasures:** public recreation areas.

250 **the holy place:** the site of the most sacred Roman temples.
251 **brands:** pieces of burning wood.

255 **forms:** benches. **windows:** shutters.

260 **Lepidus:** one of Caesar's generals.
261 **thither will . . . him:** I will go there immediately to visit him.
262 **upon a wish:** just as I had wished.

265 **Are rid:** have ridden.
266 **Belike:** probably.

1 **Cinna:** a well-known poet, not the same Cinna who helped kill Caesar.
**tonight:** last night.
2 **things . . . fantasy:** my imagination is burdened with bad omens.

**ANTONY.** Moreover, he hath left you all his walks,
His private arbors and new-planted orchards,°
245 On this side Tiber; he hath left them you,
And to your heirs forever—common pleasures,°
To walk abroad and recreate yourselves.
Here was a Caesar! when comes such another?

**FIRST PLEBEIAN.** Never, never! Come, away, away!
250 We'll burn his body in the holy place,°
And with the brands° fire the traitors' houses.
Take up the body.

**SECOND PLEBEIAN.** Go fetch fire.

**THIRD PLEBEIAN.** Pluck down benches.

255 **FOURTH PLEBEIAN.** Pluck down forms,° windows,° anything.

[*Exit* PLEBEIANS *with the body.*]

**ANTONY.** Now let it work. Mischief, thou art afoot,
Take thou what course thou wilt!

[*Enter* SERVANT.]

How now, fellow?

**SERVANT.** Sir, Octavius is already come to Rome.

**ANTONY.** Where is he?

260 **SERVANT.** He and Lepidus° are at Caesar's house.

**ANTONY.** And thither will I straight to visit him;°
He comes upon a wish.° Fortune is merry,
And in this mood will give us anything.

**SERVANT.** I heard him say, Brutus and Cassius
265 Are rid° like madmen through the gates of Rome.

**ANTONY.** Belike° they had some notice of the people,
How I had mov'd them. Bring me to Octavius.

[*They exit.*]


## SCENE 3. Shortly afterward. A street near the Forum.

[*Enter* CINNA *the poet, and after him the* PLEBEIANS.]

**CINNA.**° I dreamt tonight° that I did feast with Caesar,
And things unluckily charge my fantasy.°
I have no will to wander forth of doors,

12  **you were best:**  you had better.

18  **bear me a bang:**  get a blow from me.

Yet something leads me forth.

5    **FIRST PLEBEIAN.**   What is your name?

**SECOND PLEBEIAN.**   Whither are you going?

**THIRD PLEBEIAN.**   Where do you dwell?

**FOURTH PLEBEIAN.**   Are you a married man or a bachelor?

**SECOND PLEBEIAN.**   Answer every man directly.

10   **FIRST PLEBEIAN.**   Ay, and briefly.

**FOURTH PLEBEIAN.**   Ay, and wisely.

**THIRD PLEBEIAN.**   Ay, and truly, you were best.°

**CINNA.**   What is my name? Whither am I going? Where do I
     dwell? Am I a married man or a bachelor? Then, to answer
15   every man directly and briefly, wisely and truly: wisely I
     say, I am a bachelor.

**SECOND PLEBEIAN.**   That's as much as to say, they are fools that
     marry. You'll bear me a bang° for that, I fear. Proceed
     directly.

20   **CINNA.**   Directly, I am going to Caesar's funeral.

**FIRST PLEBEIAN.**   As a friend or an enemy?

**CINNA.**   As a friend.

**SECOND PLEBEIAN.**   That matter is answer'd directly.

**FOURTH PLEBEIAN.**   For your dwelling—briefly.

25   **CINNA.**   Briefly, I dwell by the Capitol.

**THIRD PLEBEIAN.**   Your name, sir, truly.

**CINNA.**   Truly, my name is Cinna.

**FIRST PLEBEIAN.**   Tear him to pieces, he's a conspirator.

**CINNA.**   I am Cinna the poet, I am Cinna the poet.

30   **FOURTH PLEBEIAN.**   Tear him for his bad verses, tear him for his
     bad verses.

**CINNA.**   I am not Cinna the conspirator.

**FOURTH PLEBEIAN.**   It is no matter, his name's Cinna. Pluck but
     his name out of his heart, and turn him going.

35    **THIRD PLEBEIAN.**   Tear him, tear him!
        Come, brands, ho, firebrands! To Brutus', to Cassius'; burn
        all! Some to Decius' house, and some to Casca's; some to
        Ligarius'. Away, go!

[*All the* PLEBEIANS *exit (dragging off* CINNA*).*]

1     **prick'd:** marked down on a list.

2     **Your brother . . . Lepidus:** Lepidus's brother was a prominent politician who sided with the conspirators after Caesar's assassination.

9     **cut off . . . legacies:** reduce the amount of money left to the people in Caesar's will.

13     **Meet:** fit.

14     **threefold world:** three parts of the Roman world. (In the autumn of 43 B.C., Antony, Octavius Caesar, and Lepidus formed a triumvirate—a committee of three—to rule Rome. They divided up among themselves territory that the Romans had conquered.)

15–17     **So you . . . proscription:** Octavius wonders why Antony asked Lepidus to name people who should be sentenced to death if he had so poor an opinion of him.

# Act 4

SCENE 1. **ANTONY's house in Rome. A year and a half after CAESAR's death.**

[*Enter ANTONY, OCTAVIUS, and LEPIDUS.*]

**ANTONY.**   These many then shall die, their names are prick'd.°

**OCTAVIUS.**   Your brother too must die, consent you, Lepidus?°

**LEPIDUS.**   I do consent—

**OCTAVIUS.**                    Prick him down, Antony.

**LEPIDUS.**   Upon condition Publius shall not live,
5       Who is your sister's son, Mark Antony.

**ANTONY.**   He shall not live; look, with a spot I damn him.
        But, Lepidus, go you to Caesar's house;
        Fetch the will hither, and we shall determine
        How to cut off some charge in legacies.°

10   **LEPIDUS.**   What? shall I find you here?

**OCTAVIUS.**   Or here or at the Capitol.

[*Exit LEPIDUS.*]

**ANTONY.**   This is a slight unmeritable man,
        Meet° to be sent on errands; is it fit,
        The threefold world° divided, he should stand
15       One of the three to share it?

**OCTAVIUS.**                    So you thought him,
        And took his voice who should be prick'd to die
        In our black sentence and proscription.°

**ANTONY.**   Octavius, I have seen more days than you,
        And though we lay these honors on this man

| 20 | **divers sland'rous loads:** the burden of accusations for our various actions. |
|---|---|

| 24–27 | **And having . . . commons:** When Lepidus has brought our treasure where we want it, we will send him off to shake his ears and graze on public land like an unburdened donkey. |
|---|---|

| 30 | **appoint . . . provender:** allot him a supply of food. |
|---|---|

| 32 | **wind:** turn. |
|---|---|
| 33 | **corporal:** bodily. |
| 34 | **taste:** degree. |

| 36–39 | **A barren-spirited . . . fashion:** a man with no originality, one who indulges in curiosities, tricks, and fashions, which he takes up only after they have become outmoded. |
|---|---|
| 40 | **a property:** a mere tool. |

| 41–47 | **Listen great . . . answered:** Listen to important matters. Brutus and Cassius are raising armies; we must press forward immediately. Therefore let us become united, choose our allies, and make the most of our resources. And let us decide at once how hidden threats may be uncovered and open dangers most safely confronted. |
|---|---|
| 48–49 | **we are . . . enemies:** Octavius's metaphor refers to bear-baiting, a popular entertainment in which bears were tied to stakes and surrounded by vicious dogs. |

| 20 | To ease ourselves of divers sland'rous loads,° |
| | He shall but bear them as the ass bears gold, |
| | To groan and sweat under the business, |
| | Either led or driven, as we point the way; |
| | And having brought our treasure where we will, |
| 25 | Then take we down his load, and turn him off |
| | (Like to the empty ass) to shake his ears |
| | And graze in commons.° |

**OCTAVIUS.**                    You may do your will;
But he's a tried and valiant soldier.

**ANTONY.**    So is my horse, Octavius, and for that
30    I do appoint him store of provender.°
It is a creature that I teach to fight,
To wind,° to stop, to run directly on,
His corporal° motion govern'd by my spirit;
And in some taste° is Lepidus but so.
35    He must be taught, and train'd, and bid go forth;
A barren-spirited fellow; one that feeds
On objects, arts, and imitations,
Which, out of use and stal'd by other men,
Begin his fashion.° Do not talk of him
40    But as a property.° And now, Octavius,
Listen great things. Brutus and Cassius
Are levying powers; we must straight make head;
Therefore let our alliance be combin'd,
Our best friends made, our means stretch'd;
45    And let us presently go sit in council,
How covert matters may be best disclos'd,
And open perils surest answered.°

**OCTAVIUS.**    Let us do so; for we are at the stake,
And bay'd about with many enemies,°
50    And some that smile have in their hearts, I fear,
Millions of mischiefs. [*They exit.*]

2   **Give the . . . stand:** Lucilius, one of Brutus's officers, tells his subordinates to pass on Brutus's command for the army to halt (**stand**). He has returned from Cassius's camp with Titinius, one of Cassius's officers, and Pindarus, Cassius's servant.

6–9   **Your master . . . undone:** Either a change in Cassius or the misconduct of his officers has given me good reason to wish I could undo what I have done. (Brutus is having some misgivings about having participated in the conspiracy because of incidents that have occurred in Cassius's army.)

10   **be satisfied:** receive an explanation.

14   **resolv'd:** informed.

16   **familiar instances:** signs of friendship.

17   **conference:** conversation.

21   **enforced ceremony:** strained formality.

23–27   **But hollow . . . trial:** Brutus compares insincere men to horses that are spirited at the start but drop their proud necks as soon as they feel the spur, failing like nags (**jades**) when put to the test.

29   **horse in general:** main part of the cavalry.

## SCENE 2. A military camp near Sardis in Asia Minor. Several months later.

*[Drum. Enter BRUTUS, LUCILIUS, LUCIUS, and the army. TITINIUS and PINDARUS meet them.]*

**BRUTUS.**   Stand ho!

**LUCILIUS.**   Give the word ho! and stand.°

**BRUTUS.**   What now, Lucilius, is Cassius near?

**LUCILIUS.**   He is at hand, and Pindarus is come
5      To do you salutation from his master.

**BRUTUS.**   He greets me well. Your master, Pindarus,
      In his own change, or by ill officers,
      Hath given me some worthy cause to wish
      Things done undone,° but if he be at hand,
10      I shall be satisfied.°

**PINDARUS.**            I do not doubt
      But that my noble master will appear
      Such as he is, full of regard and honor.

**BRUTUS.**   He is not doubted. A word, Lucilius.
      How he receiv'd you; let me be resolv'd.°

15   **LUCILIUS.**   With courtesy and with respect enough,
      But not with such familiar instances,°
      Nor with such free and friendly conference,°
      As he hath us'd of old.

**BRUTUS.**               Thou hast describ'd
      A hot friend cooling. Ever note, Lucilius,
20      When love begins to sicken and decay
      It useth an enforced ceremony.°
      There are no tricks in plain and simple faith;
      But hollow men, like horses hot at hand,
      Make gallant show and promise of their mettle;

*[Low march within.]*

25      But when they should endure the bloody spur,
      They fall their crests, and like deceitful jades
      Sink in the trial.° Comes his army on?

**LUCILIUS.**   They mean this night in Sardis to be quarter'd.
      The greater part, the horse in general,°
30      Are come with Cassius.

40    **sober form:** dignified manner.

42    **be content:** calm down.

47–48    **enlarge . . . audience:** Explain your grievances, and I will listen.

[*Enter* CASSIUS *and his* POWERS.]

**BRUTUS.**                 Hark! He is arriv'd.
    March gently on to meet him.

**CASSIUS.**   Stand ho!

**BRUTUS.**   Stand ho! Speak the word along.

**FIRST SOLDIER.**   Stand!

35   **SECOND SOLDIER.**   Stand!

**THIRD SOLDIER.**   Stand!

**CASSIUS.**   Most noble brother, you have done me wrong.

**BRUTUS.**   Judge me, you gods! wrong I mine enemies?
    And if not so, how should I wrong a brother.

40   **CASSIUS.**   Brutus, this sober form° of yours hides wrongs,
    And when you do them—

**BRUTUS.**   Cassius, be content.°
    Speak your griefs softly; I do know you well.
    Before the eyes of both our armies here
45     (Which should perceive nothing but love from us)
    Let us not wrangle. Bid them move away;
    Then in my tent, Cassius, enlarge your griefs,
    And I will give you audience.°

**CASSIUS.**                 Pindarus,
    Bid our commanders lead their charges off
50     A little from this ground.

**BRUTUS.**   Lucius, do you the like, and let no man
    Come to our tent till we have done our conference.
    Let Lucilius and Titinius guard our door.

[*They exit.* BRUTUS *and* CASSIUS *remain and withdraw into* BRUTUS's *tent, while*
LUCILIUS *and* TITINIUS *mount guard without.*]

**1–5** **That you . . . off:** Cassius complains that Brutus publicly disgraced (**noted**) a man for taking bribes, ignoring Cassius's request for leniency.

**7–8** **not meet . . . comment:** not fitting that each minor offense should be criticized.

**10** **condemn'd to . . . palm:** blamed for being greedy.

**11** **mart:** trade.

**15–16** **The name . . . head:** Because you have become associated with this corruption, the bribe-takers go unpunished.

**23** **supporting robbers:** Brutus now suggests that one of Caesar's offenses was to protect corrupt officials.

**28** **bait:** provoke.

**30** **hedge me in:** limit my freedom.

**32** **conditions:** regulations.

## SCENE 3. BRUTUS's tent. A few minutes later.

CASSIUS.   That you wrong'd me doth appear in this;
You have condemn'd and noted Lucius Pella
For taking bribes here of the Sardians;
Wherein my letters, praying on his side,
5   Because I knew the man, was slighted off.°

BRUTUS.   You wrong'd yourself to write in such a case.

CASSIUS.   In such a time as this it is not meet
That every nice offense should bear his comment.°

BRUTUS.   Let me tell you, Cassius, you yourself
10   Are much condemn'd to have an itching palm,°
To sell and mart° your offices for gold
To undeservers.

CASSIUS.              I, an itching palm?
You know that you are Brutus that speaks this,
Or, by the gods, this speech were else your last.

15   BRUTUS.   The name of Cassius honors this corruption,
And chastisement doth therefore hide his head.°

CASSIUS.   Chastisement?

BRUTUS.   Remember March, the ides of March remember:
Did not great Julius bleed for justice' sake?
20   What villain touch'd his body, that did stab
And not for justice? What? shall one of us,
That struck the foremost man of all this world
But for supporting robbers,° shall we now
Contaminate our fingers with base bribes?
25   And sell the mighty space of our large honors
For so much trash as may be grasped thus?
I had rather be a dog, and bay the moon,
Than such a Roman.

CASSIUS.                    Brutus, bait° not me,
I'll not endure it. You forget yourself
30   To hedge me in.° I am a soldier, I,
Older in practice, abler than yourself
To make conditions.°

BRUTUS.                    Go to; you are not, Cassius.

CASSIUS.   I am.

BRUTUS.   I say you are not.

39    **rash choler:**  quick temper.

44    **budge:**  flinch.

45    **observe you:**  defer to you.

46    **testy humor:**  irritable mood.

47–48    **digest . . . split you:**  swallow the poison of your own anger, even if it makes you burst. (The spleen was thought to be the source of anger.)

52    **vaunting:**  boasting.

54    **learn of noble men:**  learn from noble men or find out that you are noble.

58    **durst:**  dared. **mov'd:**  provoked.

64    **that:**  something that.

35  CASSIUS.  Urge me no more, I shall forget myself;
        Have mind upon your health; tempt me no farther.

    BRUTUS.  Away, slight man!

    CASSIUS.  Is't possible?

    BRUTUS.                Hear me, for I will speak.
        Must I give way and room to your rash choler?°
40      Shall I be frighted when a madman stares?

    CASSIUS.  O ye gods, ye gods, must I endure all this?

    BRUTUS.  All this? ay, more. Fret till your proud heart break.
        Go show your slaves how choleric you are,
        And make your bondmen tremble. Must I budge?°
45      Must I observe you?° Must I stand and crouch
        Under your testy humor?° By the gods,
        You shall digest the venom of your spleen
        Though it do split you;° for, from this day forth,
        I'll use you for my mirth, yea, for my laughter,
50      When you are waspish.

    CASSIUS.                Is it come to this?

    BRUTUS.  You say you are a better soldier;
        Let it appear so; make your vaunting° true,
        And it shall please me well. For mine own part,
        I shall be glad to learn of noble men.°

55  CASSIUS.  You wrong me every way; you wrong me, Brutus;
        I said, an elder soldier, not a better.
        Did I say "better"?

    BRUTUS.                If you did, I care not.

    CASSIUS.  When Caesar liv'd, he durst° not thus have mov'd° me.

    BRUTUS.  Peace, peace, you durst not so have tempted him.

60  CASSIUS.  I durst not?

    BRUTUS.  No.

    CASSIUS.  What? durst not tempt him?

    BRUTUS.                For your life you durst not.

    CASSIUS.  Do not presume too much upon my love,
        I may do that° I shall be sorry for.

65  BRUTUS.  You have done that you should be sorry for.
        There is no terror, Cassius, in your threats;

74    **vile trash:**  small sums of money.
75    **indirection:**  dishonest means.


80    **rascal counters:**  grubby coins.


85    **riv'd:**  broken.
86    **bear . . . infirmities:**  accept his friend's faults.


96    **brav'd:**  challenged.
97    **Check'd like a bondman:**  scolded like a slave.
98    **conn'd by rote:**  memorized.


102    **Pluto's mine:**  all the riches in the earth. (Pluto, the Roman god of the under-
       world, was often confused with Plutus, the god of wealth.)

For I am arm'd so strong in honesty
That they pass by me as the idle wind,
Which I respect not. I did send to you
70   For certain sums of gold, which you denied me;
For I can raise no money by vile means.
By heaven, I had rather coin my heart
And drop my blood for drachmas than to wring
From the hard hands of peasants their vile trash°
75   By any indirection.° I did send
To you for gold to pay my legions,
Which you denied me. Was that done like Cassius?
Should I have answer'd Caius Cassius so?
When Marcus Brutus grows so covetous
80   To lock such rascal counters° from his friends,
Be ready, gods, with all your thunderbolts,
Dash him to pieces!

CASSIUS.                    I denied you not.

BRUTUS.   You did.

CASSIUS.   I did not. He was but a fool that brought
85   My answer back. Brutus hath riv'd° my heart.
A friend should bear his friend's infirmities;°
But Brutus makes mine greater than they are.

BRUTUS.   I do not, till you practice them on me.

CASSIUS.   You love me not.

BRUTUS.                    I do not like your faults.

90   CASSIUS.   A friendly eye could never see such faults.

BRUTUS.   A flatterer's would not, though they do appear
As huge as high Olympus.

CASSIUS.   Come, Antony, and young Octavius, come,
Revenge yourselves alone on Cassius,
95   For Cassius is aweary of the world;
Hated by one he loves, brav'd° by his brother,
Check'd like a bondman,° all his faults observ'd,
Set in a notebook, learn'd and conn'd by rote,°
To cast into my teeth. O, I could weep
100   My spirit from mine eyes! There is my dagger,
And here my naked breast; within, a heart
Dearer than Pluto's mine,° richer than gold:
If that thou be'st a Roman, take it forth.

108–109   **Be angry . . . humor:** Brutus says that he will give Cassius's anger free play (**scope**) and will consider his insults merely the result of a bad mood.

110   **yoked:** allied.

112   **enforced:** struck hard; irritated.

113   **straight:** immediately.

115   **blood ill-temper'd:** moodiness.

121   **forgetful:** forget myself.

122–123   **When you . . . so:** When you are too difficult with me, I will attribute it to the quick temper you inherited from your mother, and leave it at that.

I, that denied thee gold, will give my heart:
105     Strike as thou didst at Caesar; for I know,
When thou didst hate him worst, thou lovedst him better
Than ever thou lovedst Cassius.

**BRUTUS.**                                Sheathe your dagger.
Be angry when you will, it shall have scope;
Do what you will, dishonor shall be humor.°
110     O Cassius, you are yoked° with a lamb
That carries anger as the flint bears fire,
Who, much enforced,° shows a hasty spark,
And straight° is cold again.

**CASSIUS.**                         Hath Cassius liv'd
To be but mirth and laughter to his Brutus
115     When grief and blood ill-temper'd° vexeth him?

**BRUTUS.**     When I spoke that, I was ill-temper'd too.

**CASSIUS.**     Do you confess so much? Give me your hand.

**BRUTUS.**     And my heart too.

**CASSIUS.**                     O Brutus!

**BRUTUS.**                             What's the matter?

**CASSIUS.**     Have you not love enough to bear with me,
120     When that rash humor which my mother gave me
Makes me forgetful?°

**BRUTUS.**                  Yes, Cassius, and from henceforth,
When you are over-earnest with your Brutus,
He'll think your mother chides, and leave you so.°

[*Enter a* POET (*to* LUCILIUS *and* TITINIUS *as they stand on guard*).]

**POET.**     Let me go in to see the generals;
125     There is some grudge between 'em; 'tis not meet
They be alone.

**LUCILIUS.**     You shall not come to them.

**POET.**     Nothing but death shall stay me.

[*BRUTUS and* CASSIUS *step out of the tent.*]

**CASSIUS.**     How now. What's the matter?

130   **POET.**     For shame, you generals! what do you mean?
Love, and be friends, as two such men should be,
For I have seen more years, I'm sure, than ye.

133     **cynic:**  rude fellow.

136     **I'll know . . . time:**  I'll accept his quirks when he learns the proper time for them.

137     **jigging:**  doggerel-making.

138     **Companion:**  fellow (used here as a term of contempt).

145–146   **Of your . . . evils:**  According to Stoicism, the philosophy Brutus studied, people should not be distressed by chance misfortunes.

150     **How scap'd I killing:**  How did I escape being killed?

151     **touching:**  painful.

152     **Impatient of:**  unable to endure.

154–155   **with her death . . . came:**  I received news of her death and of their strength at the same time.

155     **distract:**  distraught.

156     **fire:**  burning coals.

CASSIUS.   Ha, ha! how vilely doth this cynic° rhyme!

BRUTUS.   Get you hence, sirrah! saucy fellow, hence!

135 CASSIUS.   Bear with him, Brutus, 'tis his fashion.

BRUTUS.   I'll know his humor when he knows his time.°
What should the wars do with these jigging° fools?
Companion,° hence!

CASSIUS.                              Away, away, be gone! [*Exit* POET.]

BRUTUS.   Lucilius and Titinius, bid the commanders
140     Prepare to lodge their companies tonight.

CASSIUS.   And come yourselves, and bring Messala with you
Immediately to us.

[*LUCILIUS and* TITINIUS *exit.*]

BRUTUS.   [*To* LUCIUS *within.*] Lucius, a bowl of wine!

[*BRUTUS and* CASSIUS *return into the tent.*]

CASSIUS.   I did not think you could have been so angry.

BRUTUS.   O Cassius, I am sick of many griefs.

145 CASSIUS.   Of your philosophy you make no use,
If you give place to accidental evils.°

BRUTUS.   No man bears sorrow better. Portia is dead.

CASSIUS.   Ha? Portia?

BRUTUS.   She is dead.

150 CASSIUS.   How scap'd I killing° when I cross'd you so?
O insupportable and touching° loss!
Upon what sickness?

BRUTUS.                              Impatient of° my absence,
And grief that young Octavius with Mark Antony
Have made themselves so strong—for with her death
155     That tidings came.° With this she fell distract,°
And (her attendants absent) swallow'd fire.°

CASSIUS.   And died so?

BRUTUS.                              Even so.

CASSIUS.                              O ye immortal gods!

[*Enter Boy (*LUCIUS*) with wine and tapers.*]

BRUTUS.   Speak no more of her. Give me a bowl of wine.
In this I bury all unkindness, Cassius. [*Drinks.*]

165    **call . . . necessities:**  discuss what we must do.


169    **power:**  army.

170    **Bending . . . Philippi:**  Directing their march toward Philippi (an ancient town in northern Greece).

171    **tenure:**  basic meaning.


173    **proscription:**  condemning to death.

160 CASSIUS.   My heart is thirsty for that noble pledge.
　　　　Fill, Lucius, till the wine o'erswell the cup;
　　　　I cannot drink too much of Brutus' love.

[*Drinks. Exit* LUCIUS.]

　　BRUTUS.   Come in, Titinius. [*Enter* TITINIUS *and* MESSALA.]
　　　　Welcome, good Messala.
　　　　Now sit we close about this taper here,
165　　And call in question our necessities.°

　　CASSIUS.   Portia, art thou gone?

　　BRUTUS.                              No more, I pray you.
　　　　Messala, I have here received letters
　　　　That young Octavius and Mark Antony
　　　　Come down upon us with a mighty power,°
170　　Bending their expedition toward Philippi.°

　　MESSALA.   Myself have letters of the selfsame tenure.°

　　BRUTUS.   With what addition?

　　MESSALA.   That by proscription° and bills of outlawry
　　　　Octavius, Antony, and Lepidus
175　　Have put to death an hundred senators.

　　BRUTUS.   Therein our letters do not well agree;
　　　　Mine speak of seventy senators that died
　　　　By their proscriptions, Cicero being one.

　　CASSIUS.   Cicero one?

　　MESSALA.               Cicero is dead,
180　　And by that order of proscription.
　　　　Had you your letters from your wife, my lord?

　　BRUTUS.   No, Messala.

　　MESSALA.   Nor nothing in your letters writ of her?

　　BRUTUS.   Nothing, Messala.

　　MESSALA.                    That methinks is strange.

185 BRUTUS.   Why ask you? Hear you aught of her in yours?

　　MESSALA.   No, my lord.

　　BRUTUS.   Now as you are a Roman, tell me true.

　　MESSALA.   Then like a Roman bear the truth I tell,
　　　　For certain she is dead, and by strange manner.

190 BRUTUS.   Why, farewell, Portia. We must die, Messala.

| 181–195 | **Had you your . . . bear it so:** This passage contradicts lines 147–158, where Brutus tells Cassius of Portia's death. Many scholars believe that the second passage was mistakenly printed in a revised version of the play. According to this theory, Shakespeare originally emphasized Brutus's philosophical composure, but in rewriting the play, he decided to offer a warmer view of Brutus grieving for his wife. |
|---|---|
| 191 | **once:** at some time. |
| 194–195 | **I have as . . . so:** Cassius says that although he shares Brutus's ideal of philosophical self-control, he could not practice it as Brutus does. |
| 196 | **alive:** at hand or of the living. |
| 200 | **waste his means:** use up his supplies. |
| 201 | **Doing himself offense:** harming himself. |
| 205 | **Do stand . . . affection:** Are friendly toward us only because they have no choice. |
| 209 | **new-added:** reinforced. |
| 213 | **Under your pardon:** I beg your pardon (let me continue). |
| 214 | **tried . . . friends:** demanded from our allies all that they can give. |
| 215 | **brimful:** at full strength. |
| 218–221 | **There is a . . . miseries:** Brutus says that if men fail to act when the tide of fortune is flowing, they may never get another opportunity. |
| 224 | **with your will:** as you wish. |

With meditating that she must die once,°
I have the patience to endure it now.

MESSALA.    Even so great men great losses should endure.

CASSIUS.    I have as much of this in art as you,
195    But yet my nature could not bear it so.°

BRUTUS.    Well, to our work alive.° What do you think
Of marching to Philippi presently?

CASSIUS.    I do not think it good.

BRUTUS.                                    Your reason?

CASSIUS.                                                        This it is;
'Tis better that the enemy seek us;
200    So shall he waste his means,° weary his soldiers,
Doing himself offense,° whilst we, lying still,
Are full of rest, defense, and nimbleness.

BRUTUS.    Good reasons must of force give place to better:
The people 'twixt Philippi and this ground
205    Do stand but in a forc'd affection;°
For they have grudg'd us contribution.
The enemy, marching along by them,
By them shall make a fuller number up,
Come on refresh'd, new-added° and encourag'd;
210    From which advantage shall we cut him off
If at Philippi we do face him there,
These people at our back.

CASSIUS.                                    Here me, good brother.

BRUTUS.    Under your pardon.° You must note beside
That we have tried the utmost of our friends,°
215    Our legions are brimful,° our cause is ripe:
The enemy increaseth every day;
We, at the height, are ready to decline.
There is a tide in the affairs of men,
Which, taken at the flood, leads on to fortune;
220    Omitted, all the voyage of their life
Is bound in shallows and in miseries.°
On such a full sea are we now afloat,
And we must take the current when it serves,
Or lose our ventures.

CASSIUS.                            Then with your will° go on;
225    We'll along ourselves, and meet them at Philippi.

227–228 **nature must . . . rest:** Human nature has its needs, which we will grudgingly satisfy (**niggard**) by resting briefly.

241 **knave:** lad. **o'erwatch'd:** tired from staying awake too long.

247 **raise:** awaken.

249 **stand . . . pleasure:** stay awake and be ready to serve you.

**BRUTUS.** The deep of night is crept upon our talk,
And nature must obey necessity,
Which we will niggard with a little rest.°
There is no more to say?

**CASSIUS.** No more. Good night.
230 Early tomorrow will we rise, and hence.

**BRUTUS.** Lucius. [*Enter* LUCIUS.] My gown. [*Exit* LUCIUS.]
Farewell, good Messala.
Good night, Titinius. Noble, noble Cassius,
Good night, and good repose.

**CASSIUS.** O my dear brother!
This was an ill beginning of the night.
235 Never come such division 'tween our souls!
Let it not, Brutus.

[*Enter* LUCIUS *with the gown.*]

**BRUTUS.** Everything is well.

**CASSIUS.** Good night, my lord.

**BRUTUS.** Good night, good brother.

**TITINIUS AND MESSALA.** Good night, Lord Brutus.

**BRUTUS.** Farewell
every one.

[*Exit (all but* BRUTUS *and* LUCIUS*).*]

Give me the gown. Where is thy instrument?

240 **LUCIUS.** Here in the tent.

**BRUTUS.** What, thou speak'st drowsily?
Poor knave,° I blame thee not; thou art o'erwatch'd.°
Call Claudio and some other of my men,
I'll have them sleep on cushions in my tent.

**LUCIUS.** Varrus and Claudio!

[*Enter* VARRUS *and* CLAUDIO.]

245 **VARRUS.** Calls my lord?

**BRUTUS.** I pray you, sirs, lie in my tent and sleep;
It may be I shall raise° you by and by
On business to my brother Cassius.

**VARRUS.** So please you, we will stand and watch your pleasure.°

250 **BRUTUS.** I will not have it so. Lie down, good sirs,

251 **It may be . . . me:** I might change my mind.

257 **touch thy . . . two:** play a song or two. (Lucius probably plays the lute, a stringed instrument.)
258 **an't:** if it.

267–268 **O murd'rous . . . mace:** Officers used to touch a rod (**mace**) to a person's shoulder as a sign of arrest. Brutus calls the mace of deathlike (**murd'rous**) sleep "leaden" because of its heaviness.

275 **How ill . . . burns:** It was believed that candles burn dimly when a ghost appears.

280 **stare:** stand on end.

It may be I shall otherwise bethink me.°

[*VARRUS and* CLAUDIO *lie down.*]

> Look, Lucius, here's the book I sought for so;
> I put it in the pocket of my gown.

LUCIUS.   I was sure your lordship did not give it me.

255   BRUTUS.   Bear with me, good boy, I am much forgetful.
> Canst thou hold up thy heavy eyes awhile,
> And touch thy instrument a strain or two?°

LUCIUS.   Ay, my lord, an't° please you.

BRUTUS.                           It does, my boy.
> I trouble thee too much, but thou are willing.

260   LUCIUS.   It is my duty, sir.

BRUTUS.   I should not urge thy duty past thy might;
> I know young bloods look for a time of rest.

LUCIUS.   I have slept, my lord, already.

BRUTUS.   It was well done, and thou shalt sleep again;
265   I will not hold thee long. If I do live,
> I will be good to thee.

[*Music, and a song.*]

> This is a sleepy tune. O murd'rous slumber!
> Layest thou thy leaden mace° upon my boy,
> That plays thee music? Gentle knave, good night;
270   I will not do thee so much wrong to wake thee.
> If thou dost nod, thou break'st thy instrument;
> I'll take it from thee; and, good boy, good night.
> Let me see, let me see; is not the leaf turn'd down
> Where I left reading? Here it is, I think.

[*Enter the* GHOST OF CAESAR.]

275   How ill this taper burns!° Ha! who comes here?
> I think it is the weakness of mine eyes
> That shapes this monstrous apparition.
> It comes upon me. Art thou anything?
> Art thou some god, some angel, or some devil,
280   That mak'st my blood cold, and my hair to stare?°
> Speak to me what thou art.

GHOST.   Thy evil spirit, Brutus.

291    **false:**  out of tune.

306    **commend me:**  send my regards.
307    **set on . . . before:**  start his troops moving early, at the lead.

**BRUTUS.** Why com'st thou?

**GHOST.** To tell thee thou shalt see me at Philippi.

**BRUTUS.** Well; then I shall see thee again?

285 **GHOST.** Ay, at Philippi.

**BRUTUS.** Why, I will see thee at Philippi then.

[*Exit* GHOST.]

Now I have taken heart thou vanishest.
Ill spirit, I would hold more talk with thee.
Boy! Lucius! Varrus! Claudio! Sirs, awake!
290 Claudio!

**LUCIUS.** The strings, my lord, are false.°

**BRUTUS.** He thinks he still is at his instrument.
Lucius, awake!

**LUCIUS.** My lord?

295 **BRUTUS.** Didst thou dream, Lucius, that thou so criedst out?

**LUCIUS.** My lord, I do not know that I did cry.

**BRUTUS.** Yes, that thou didst. Didst thou see anything?

**LUCIUS.** Nothing, my lord.

**BRUTUS.** Sleep again, Lucius. Sirrah Claudio!

300 [*To* CLAUDIO *and then* VARRUS.] Fellow thou, awake!

**VARRUS.** My lord?

**CLAUDIO.** My lord?

**BRUTUS.** Why did you so cry out, sirs, in your sleep?

**BOTH.** Did we, my lord?

**BRUTUS.** Ay. Saw you anything?

305 **VARRUS.** No, my lord, I saw nothing.

**CLAUDIO.** Nor I, my lord.

**BRUTUS.** Go and commend me° to my brother Cassius;
Bid him set on his pow'rs betimes before,°
And we will follow.

**BOTH.** It shall be done, my lord.

[*They exit.*]

4    **battles:** armies.

5    **warn:** defy.

6    **Answering before . . . them:** responding with hostility before we even challenge them to fight.

7    **am in their bosoms:** know what is in their hearts.

8–11    **They could . . . courage:** Antony dismisses his enemy's bravery as a false show (**face**), saying that they would really prefer to be somewhere else.

10    **fearful:** frightening or full of fear.

14    **bloody sign:** A red flag was flown from a Roman general's tent to signal the start of battle.

16    **softly:** slowly.

17    **even:** level.

19    **cross me in this exigent:** oppose me at this moment of crisis.

20    **I will do so:** I will do as I said. (Octavius insists on attacking from the right, which is usually the position of the most experienced general.)

# Act 5

**SCENE 1. The Plains of Philippi in Greece. A few weeks later.**

[*Enter* OCTAVIUS, ANTONY, *and their* ARMY.]

    **OCTAVIUS.**   Now, Antony, our hopes are answered.
      You said the enemy would not come down,
      But keep the hills and upper regions.
      It proves not so: their battles° are at hand;
5      They mean to warn° us at Philippi here,
      Answering before we do demand of them.°

    **ANTONY.**   Tut, I am in their bosoms,° and I know
      Wherefore they do it. They could be content
      To visit other places, and come down
10     With fearful° bravery, thinking by this face
      To fasten in our thoughts that they have courage;°
      But 'tis not so.

[*Enter a* MESSENGER.]

    **MESSENGER.**      Prepare you, generals,
      The enemy comes on in gallant show;
      Their bloody sign° of battle is hung out,
15     And something to be done immediately.

    **ANTONY.**   Octavius, lead your battle softly° on
      Upon the left hand of the even° field.

    **OCTAVIUS.**   Upon the right hand I, keep thou the left.

    **ANTONY.**   Why do you cross me in this exigent?°

20    **OCTAVIUS.**   I do not cross you; but I will do so.° [*March.*]

21    **would have parley:** request a conference.

24    **answer on their charge:** respond when they attack.

33    **The posture . . . unknown:** We don't know what kind of blows you will strike.

34    **Hybla:** an area in Sicily noted for its honey. (Cassius is reminding Antony of his "sweet" words to the conspirators after the assassination.)

41    **show'd your [teeth]:** grinned.

47    **If Cassius . . . rul'd:** if Cassius had had his way (when he argued that Antony should be killed).

48    **cause:** business at hand.

49    **The proof of it:** deciding the argument in battle.

52    **goes up again:** goes back into its sheath.

[*Drum. Enter* BRUTUS, CASSIUS, *and their* ARMY; LUCILIUS, TITINIUS, MESSALA, *and others*.]

**BRUTUS.**   They stand, and would have parley.°

**CASSIUS.**   Stand fast, Titinius; we must out and talk.

**OCTAVIUS.**   Mark Antony, shall we give sign of battle?

**ANTONY.**   No, Caesar, we will answer on their charge.°
25      Make forth, the generals would have some words.

**OCTAVIUS.**   Stir not until the signal.

**BRUTUS.**   Words before blows; is it so, countrymen?

**OCTAVIUS.**   Not that we love words better, as you do.

**BRUTUS.**   Good words are better than bad strokes, Octavius.

30   **ANTONY.**   In your bad strokes, Brutus, you give good words;
        Witness the hole you made in Caesar's heart,
        Crying, "Long live! hail, Caesar!"

**CASSIUS.**                                         Antony,
        The posture of your blows are yet unknown;°
        But for your words, they rob the Hybla° bees,
35      And leave them honeyless.

**ANTONY.**                              Not stingless too?

**BRUTUS.**   O, yes, and soundless too;
        For you have stol'n their buzzing, Antony,
        And very wisely threat before you sting.

**ANTONY.**   Villains! you did not so, when your vile daggers
40      Hack'd one another in the sides of Caesar.
        You show'd your [teeth]° like apes, and fawn'd like hounds,
        And bow'd like bondmen, kissing Caesar's feet;
        Whilst damned Casca, like a cur, behind
        Struck Caesar on the neck. O you flatterers!

45   **CASSIUS.**   Flatterers? Now, Brutus, thank yourself;
        This tongue had not offended so today,
        If Cassius might have rul'd.°

**OCTAVIUS.**   Come, come, the cause.° If arguing make us sweat,
        The proof of it° will turn to redder drops.
50      Look,
        I draw a sword against conspirators;
        When think you that the sword goes up again?°
        Never, till Caesar's three and thirty wounds

**54–55**  **till another . . . traitors:** until the conspirators have killed another Caesar (that is, Octavius himself).

**56–57**  **Caesar . . . thee:** Brutus suggests that all the traitors are on the side of Octavius and Antony.

**59**  **strain:** family.

**61**  **schoolboy:** Octavius was twenty-one at the time of the battle.

**62**  **a masker and a reveler:** one who indulges in lavish entertainment and drunken feasts.

**66**  **stomachs:** appetite for battle.

**68**  **all is . . . hazard:** Everything is at stake.

**74**  **As Pompey was:** Pompey was persuaded against his better judgment to fight at Pharsalus, where he was defeated by Caesar.

**76**  **held Epicurus strong:** have been a firm believer in Epicurus (a Greek philosopher whose followers did not believe in omens).

**78**  **presage:** foretell the future.

**79**  **former ensign:** foremost banner.

**82**  **consorted:** accompanied.

Be well aveng'd; or till another Caesar
55  Have added slaughter to the sword of traitors.°

**BRUTUS.**   Caesar, thou canst not die by traitors' hands,   — *Period 2*
Unless thou bring'st them with thee.°

**OCTAVIUS.**                              So I hope;
I was not born to die on Brutus' sword.

**BRUTUS.**   O, if thou wert the noblest of thy strain,°
60  Young man, thou couldst not die more honorable.

**CASSIUS.**   A peevish schoolboy,° worthless of such honor,
Join'd with a masker and a reveler!°

**ANTONY.**   Old Cassius still!

**OCTAVIUS.**                              Come, Antony; away!
Defiance, traitors, hurl we in your teeth.
65  If you dare fight today, come to the field;
If not, when you have stomachs.°

[*Exit* OCTAVIUS, ANTONY, *and* ARMY.]

**CASSIUS.**   Why, now blow wind, swell billow, and swim bark!
The storm is up, and all is on the hazard.°

**BRUTUS.**   Ho, Lucilius, hark, a word with you.

[*LUCILIUS and (then)* MESSALA *stand forth.*]

**LUCILIUS.**                              My lord?

[*BRUTUS and* LUCILIUS *converse apart.*]

70  **CASSIUS.**   Messala!

**MESSALA.**            What says my general?

**CASSIUS.**                              Messala,
This is my birthday; as this very day
Was Cassius born. Give me thy hand, Messala;
Be thou my witness that against my will
(As Pompey was)° am I compell'd to set
75  Upon one battle all our liberties.
You know that I held Epicurus strong,°
And his opinion; now I change my mind,
And partly credit things that do presage.°
Coming from Sardis, on our former ensign°
80  Two mighty eagles fell, and there they perch'd,
Gorging and feeding from our soldiers' hands,
Who to Philippi here consorted° us.

**84**   **kites:**  hawks. (All three birds are scavengers, considered omens of death.)

**86**   **As:**  As if.

**91**   **constantly:**  resolutely.

**92**   **Even so, Lucilius:**  Brutus finishes his discussion with Lucilius.

**93–94**   **The gods . . . age:**  May the gods remain friendly today, so that we, dear friends in peace with each other, may live to see old age.

**96**   **Let's reason . . . befall:**  Let's consider the worst that can happen.

**100–107**   **Even by the . . . below:**  Brutus says that according to his beliefs, suicide is cowardly (he refers to his father-in-law, Cato, who killed himself after Caesar's defeat of Pompey). He would endure his fate rather than cut short (**prevent**) his life because of what might happen.

**110–112**   **Think not . . . mind:**  Brutus is suggesting that even though he rejects suicide, his pride would force him to commit such an act rather than allow himself to be paraded through the streets of Rome.

This morning are they fled away and gone,
And in their steads do ravens, crows, and kites°
85 Fly o'er our heads, and downward look on us
As° we were sickly prey. Their shadows seem
A canopy most fatal, under which
Our army lies, ready to give up the ghost.

**MESSALA.**   Believe not so.

**CASSIUS.**                                          I but believe it partly,
90 For I am fresh of spirit, and resolv'd
To meet all perils very constantly.°

**BRUTUS.**   Even so, Lucilius.°

**CASSIUS.**                                          Now, most noble Brutus,
The gods today stand friendly, that we may,
Lovers in peace, lead on our days to age!°
95 But since the affairs of men rest still incertain,
Let's reason with the worst that may befall.°
If we do lose this battle, then is this
The very last time we shall speak together:
What are you then determined to do?

100 **BRUTUS.**   Even by the rule of that philosophy
By which I did blame Cato for the death
Which he did give himself—I know not how,
But I do find it cowardly and vile,
For fear of what might fall, so to prevent
105 The time of life—arming myself with patience
To stay the providence of some high powers
That govern us below.°

**CASSIUS.**                                          Then, if we lose this battle,
You are contented to be led in triumph
Thorough the streets of Rome?

110 **BRUTUS.**   No, Cassius, no. Think not, thou noble Roman,
That ever Brutus will go bound to Rome;
He bears too great a mind.° But this same day
Must end that work the ides of March begun.
And whether we shall meet again I know not;
115 Therefore our everlasting farewell take:
Forever, and forever, farewell, Cassius!
If we do meet again, why, we shall smile;
If not, why then this parting was well made.

1   **bills:**  written orders.
2   **legions on . . . side:**  other wing of troops (led by Cassius).


4   **cold demeanor:**  lack of spirit.


1   **villains:**  Cassius's own troops (who are retreating).
2   **Myself have . . . enemy:**  I have turned to fighting my own men.
3   **ensign:**  standard bearer.
4   **it:**  the standard, or army flag.


7   **spoil:**  looting.


10  **tents:**  camp.

**CASSIUS.**   Forever, and forever, farewell, Brutus!
120         If we do meet again, we'll smile indeed;
            If not 'tis true this parting was well made.

**BRUTUS.**   Why then, lead on. O, that a man might know
            The end of this day's business ere it come!
            But it sufficeth that the day will end,
125         And then the end is known. Come, ho, away!

[*BRUTUS, CASSIUS, and their ARMY withdraw to begin the battle.*]


## SCENE 2. The field of battle. Shortly afterward.

[*Alarm. Enter BRUTUS and MESSALA.*]

**BRUTUS.**   Ride, ride, Messala, ride, and give these bills°
            Unto the legions on the other side.°

[*Loud alarm.*]

            Let them set on at once; for I perceive
            But cold demeanor° in Octavio's wing,
5          And sudden push gives them the overthrow.
            Ride, ride, Messala, let them all come down.

[*They exit.*]


## SCENE 3. Another part of the battlefield. Several hours later.

[*Alarms. Enter CASSIUS and TITINIUS.*]

**CASSIUS.**   O, look, Titinius, look, the villains° fly!
            Myself have to mine own turn'd enemy.°
            This ensign° here of mine was turning back;
            I slew the coward, and did take it° from him.

5   **TITINIUS.**   O Cassius, Brutus gave the word too early,
            Who, having some advantage on Octavius,
            Took it too eagerly. His soldiers fell to spoil,°
            Whilst we by Antony are all enclos'd.

[*Enter PINDARUS.*]

**PINDARUS.**   Fly further off, my lord, fly further off;
10         Mark Antony is in your tents,° my lord;
            Fly, therefore, noble Cassius, fly far off.

15    **hide:** dig.

19    **even with a thought:** as quick as a thought.

21    **my sight . . . thick:** I have always been nearsighted.

25    **is run his compass:** has come full circle.

29    **make to . . . spur:** ride quickly toward him.

31    **some light:** some of them dismount.

32    **ta'en:** taken prisoner.

38    **swore thee . . . life:** made you swear when I saved your life.

42    **search:** penetrate.
43    **Stand not:** don't wait. **hilts:** sword handles.

CASSIUS.    This hill is far enough. Look, look, Titinius!
Are those my tents where I perceive the fire?

TITINIUS.    They are, my lord.

CASSIUS.                                Titinius, if thou lovest me,
15      Mount thou my horse, and hide° thy spurs in him
Till he have brought thee up to yonder troops.
And here again, that I may rest assur'd
Whether yond troops are friend or enemy.

TITINIUS.    I will be here again, even with a thought.°

[*Exit.*]

20    CASSIUS.    Go, Pindarus, get higher on that hill;
My sight was ever thick;° regard Titinius,
And tell me what thou not'st about the field.

[*PINDARUS goes up.*]

This day I breathed first: time is come round,
And where I did begin, there shall I end;
25      My life is run his compass.° Sirrah, what news?

PINDARUS.    [*Above.*] O my lord!

CASSIUS.    What news?

PINDARUS.    Titinius is enclosed round about
With horsemen, that make to him on the spur,°
30      Yet he spurs on. Now they are almost on him.
Now, Titinius! Now some light.° O, he lights too!
He's ta'en!° [*Shout.*] And, hark, they shout for joy.

CASSIUS.    Come down; behold no more.
O, coward that I am, to live so long,
35      To see my best friend ta'en° before my face!

[*PINDARUS descends.*]

Come hither, sirrah.
In Parthia did I take thee prisoner,
And then I swore thee, saving of thy life,°
That whatsoever I did bid thee do,
40      Thou shouldst attempt it. Come now, keep thine oath;
Now be a freeman, and with this good sword,
That ran through Caesar's bowels, search° this bosom.
Stand not° to answer; here, take thou the hilts,°
And when my face is cover'd, as 'tis now,

51    **change:**  an even exchange of fortune. (Pindarus was mistaken when he
      reported Titinius's capture; Titinius had in fact come upon Brutus's troops.)

64    **dews:**  Dews were considered unhealthy.
65    **Mistrust of my success:**  Fear of my mission's outcome.
66    **Mistrust of good success:**  Fear of how the battle would turn out.
67    **O hateful . . . child:**  Messala suggests that Cassius's melancholy tempera-
      ment caused him to misperceive events.
68    **apt:**  ready (to be deceived).

71    **the mother . . . thee:**  the mind that conceived the error.

76    **darts:**  arrows.

45       Guide thou the sword. [*PINDARUS stabs him.*] Caesar, thou art
           reveng'd,
      Even with the sword that kill'd thee. [*Dies.*]

**PINDARUS.**    So, I am free; yet would not so have been,
      Durst I have done my will. O Cassius,
      Far from this country Pindarus shall run,
50       Where never Roman shall take note of him. [*Exit.*]

[*Enter TITINIUS and MESSALA.*]

**MESSALA.**    It is but change,° Titinius; for Octavius
      Is overthrown by noble Brutus' power,
      As Cassius' legions are by Antony.

**TITINIUS.**    These tidings will well comfort Cassius.

55   **MESSALA.**    Where did you leave him?

**TITINIUS.**                    All disconsolate,
      With Pindarus his bondman, on this hill.

**MESSALA.**    Is not that he that lies upon the ground?

**TITINIUS.**    He lies not like the living. O my heart!

**MESSALA.**    Is not that he?

**TITINIUS.**               No, this was he, Messala,
60       But Cassius is no more. O setting sun,
      As in thy red rays thou dost sink tonight,
      So in his red blood Cassius' day is set!
      The sun of Rome is set. Our day is gone,
      Clouds, dews,° and dangers come; our deeds are done!
65       Mistrust of my success° hath done this deed.

**MESSALA.**    Mistrust of good success° hath done this deed.
      O hateful error, melancholy's child,°
      Why dost thou show to the apt° thoughts of men
      The things that are not? O error, soon conceiv'd,
70       Thou never com'st unto a happy birth,
      But kill'st the mother that engend'red thee!°

**TITINIUS.**    What, Pindarus? Where art thou, Pindarus?

**MESSALA.**    Seek him, Titinius, whilst I go to meet
      The noble Brutus, thrusting this report
75       Into his ears; I may say "thrusting" it;
      For piercing steel and darts° envenomed
      Shall be as welcome to the ears of Brutus
      As tidings of this sight.

87  **apace:** quickly.

88  **regarded:** honored.

89  **By your . . . part:** Titinius asks the gods to pardon him because he is cutting his life short to fulfill a Roman's duty (**part**).

93  **Cato:** Brutus's brother-in-law, the son of Marcus Cato.

96  **our own proper:** our very own.

97  **Look . . . crown'd:** see how he has crowned.

101  **fellow:** equal. **moe:** more.

104  **Thasos:** an island near Philippi.

106  **discomfort:** dishearten.

**TITINIUS.**                    Hie you, Messala,
       And I will seek for Pindarus the while.

[*Exit* MESSALA.]

80       Why didst thou send me forth, brave Cassius?
         Did I not meet thy friends? and did not they
         Put on my brows this wreath of victory,
         And bid me give it thee? Didst thou not hear their shouts?
         Alas, thou hast misconstrued everything.
85       But hold thee, take this garland on thy brow;
         Thy Brutus bid me give it thee, and I
         Will do his bidding. Brutus, come apace,°
         And see how I regarded° Caius Cassius.
         By your leave, gods!—this is a Roman's part;°
90       Come, Cassius' sword, and find Titinius' heart. [*Dies.*]

[*Alarm. Enter* BRUTUS, MESSALA, LUCILIUS, VOLUMNIUS, YOUNG CATO, *and* STRATO.]

**BRUTUS.**    Where, where, Messala, doth his body lie?

**MESSALA.**    Lo, yonder, and Titinius mourning it.

**BRUTUS.**    Titinius' face is upward.

**CATO.**°                          He is slain.

**BRUTUS.**    O Julius Caesar, thou art mighty yet!
95       Thy spirit walks abroad, and turns our swords
         In our own proper° entrails. [*Low alarms.*]

**CATO.**                          Brave Titinius!
         Look, whe'er he have not crown'd° dead Cassius!

**BRUTUS.**    Are yet two Romans living such as these?
         The last of all the Romans, fare thee well!
100      It is impossible that ever Rome
         Should breed thy fellow.° Friends, I owe moe° tears
         To this dead man than you shall see me pay.
         I shall find time, Cassius; I shall find time.
         Come, therefore, and to Thasos° send his body;
105      His funerals shall not be in our camp,
         Lest it discomfort° us. Lucilius, come,
         And come, young Cato; let us to the field.
         Labio and Flavio set our battles on.
         'Tis three a'clock; and, Romans, yet ere night
110      We shall try fortune in a second fight.

[*They exit.*]

1     **Yet . . . heads:** Brutus urges his troops to keep fighting.

2     **What bastard doth not:** Who among us was born so low that he doesn't?

4     **Marcus Cato:** Portia's father.

7–8     **And I am . . . Brutus:** Lucilius impersonates his leader to divert the enemy's attention from the real Brutus.

13     **There is . . . straight:** You have good reason to kill me immediately.

24     **or . . . or:** either . . . or.

25     **like himself:** behaving like his noble self.

# SCENE 4. Another part of the battlefield. Shortly thereafter.

[*Alarm. Enter* BRUTUS, MESSALA, (*young*) CATO, LUCILIUS, *and* FLAVIUS.]

**BRUTUS.** Yet, countrymen, O, yet hold up your heads!° [*They exit.*]

**CATO.** What bastard doth not?° Who will go with me?
I will proclaim my name about the field.
I am the son of Marcus Cato,° ho!
5 A foe to tyrants, and my country's friend.
I am the son of Marcus Cato, ho!

[*Enter* SOLDIERS *and fight.*]

**LUCILIUS.** And I am Brutus, Marcus Brutus, I;
Brutus, my country's friend; know me for Brutus!°

[YOUNG CATO *is slain.*]

O young and noble Cato, art thou down?
10 Why, now thou diest as bravely as Titinius,
And mayst be honor'd, being Cato's son.

**FIRST SOLDIER.** Yield, or thou diest.

**LUCILIUS.** Only I yield to die;
There is so much that thou wilt kill me straight:°
Kill Brutus, and be honor'd in his death.

15 **FIRST SOLDIER.** We must not. A noble prisoner!

[*Enter* ANTONY.]

**SECOND SOLDIER.** Room, ho! Tell Antony, Brutus is ta'en.

**FIRST SOLDIER.** I'll tell the news. Here comes the general.
Brutus is ta'en. Brutus is ta'en, my lord.

**ANTONY.** Where is he?

20 **LUCILIUS.** Safe, Antony, Brutus is safe enough.
I dare assure thee that no enemy
Shall ever take alive the noble Brutus;
The gods defend him from so great a shame!
When you do find him, or alive or° dead,
25 He will be found like Brutus, like himself.°

**ANTONY.** This is not Brutus, friend, but, I assure you,
A prize no less in worth. Keep this man safe,
Give him all kindness; I had rather have
Such men my friends than enemies. Go on,

30 **whe'er:** whether.

2 **Statilius:** a soldier sent out to see if all is well, and if so, to signal by torchlight.

5 **It is . . . fashion:** So many are being killed.

15 **list:** hear.

18 **several:** separate.

22 **Thou seest . . . goes:** You see how things are going.
23 **pit:** a hole into which hunted animals are driven (also, a grave).

30      And see whe'er° Brutus be alive or dead,
        And bring us word unto Octavius' tent
        How everything is chanc'd.

[*They exit.*]


# SCENE 5. Another part of the field. Late in the day.

[*Enter* BRUTUS, CLITUS, DARDANIUS, VOLUMNIUS, *and* STRATO.]

**BRUTUS.**    Come, poor remains of friends, rest on this rock.

**CLITUS.**    Statilius° show'd the torchlight, but, my lord,
        He came not back. He is or ta'en or slain.

**BRUTUS.**    Sit thee down, Clitus; slaying is the word,
5       It is a deed in fashion.° Hark thee, Clitus. [*Whispering.*]

**CLITUS.**    What, I, my lord? No, not for all the world.

**BRUTUS.**    Peace then, no words.

**CLITUS.**                                    I'll rather kill myself.

**BRUTUS.**    Hark thee, Dardanius. [*Whispering.*]

**DARDANIUS.**                            Shall I do such a deed?

**CLITUS.**    O Dardanius!

10      **DARDANIUS.**    O Clitus!

**CLITUS.**    What ill request did Brutus make to thee?

**DARDANIUS.**    To kill him, Clitus. Look, he meditates.

**CLITUS.**    Now is that noble vessel full of grief,
        That it runs over even at his eyes.

15      **BRUTUS.**    Come hither, good Volumnius; list° a word.

**VOLUMNIUS.**    What says my lord?

**BRUTUS.**                            Why, this, Volumnius;
        The ghost of Caesar hath appear'd to me
        Two several° times by night; at Sardis once,
        And this last night, here in Philippi fields.
20      I know my hour is come.

**VOLUMNIUS.**                        Not so, my lord.

**BRUTUS.**    Nay, I am sure it is, Volumnius.
        Thou seest the world, Volumnius, how it goes;°
        Our enemies have beat us to the pit.°

[*Low alarms.*]

29    **office:** job.

34    **joy:** rejoice.

35    **no man . . . me:** no man to be unfaithful to me.

36–38    **I shall . . . unto:** I shall have more glory from this defeat than Octavius and Antony will achieve from their ignoble victory.

45    **respect:** reputation.

46    **smatch:** taste.

It is more worthy to leap in ourselves
25 Than tarry till they push us. Good Volumnius,
Thou know'st that we two went to school together;
Even for that our love of old, I prithee
Hold thou my sword-hilts, whilst I run on it.

**VOLUMNIUS.** That's not an office° for a friend, my lord.

[*Alarm still.*]

30 **CLITUS.** Fly, fly, my lord, there is no tarrying here.

**BRUTUS.** Farewell to you, and you, and you, Volumnius.
Strato, thou hast been all this while asleep;
Farewell to thee too, Strato. Countrymen,
My heart doth joy° that yet in all my life
35 I found no man but he was true to me.°
I shall have glory by this losing day
More than Octavius and Mark Antony
By this vile conquest shall attain unto.°
So fare you well at once, for Brutus' tongue
40 Hath almost ended his life's history.
Night hangs upon mine eyes; my bones would rest,
That have but labor'd to attain this hour.

[*Alarm. Cry within, "Fly, fly, fly!"*]

**CLITUS.** Fly, my lord, fly!

**BRUTUS.**                    Hence! I will follow.

[*CLITUS, DARDANIUS, and VOLUMNIUS exit.*]

I prithee, Strato, stay thou by thy lord,
45 Thou art a fellow of a good respect;°
Thy life hath had some smatch° of honor in it.
Hold then my sword, and turn away thy face,
While I do run upon it. Wilt thou, Strato?

**STRATO.** Give me your hand first. Fare you well, my lord.

50 **BRUTUS.** Farewell, good Strato. [*Runs on his sword.*] Caesar,
now be still,
I kill'd not thee with half so good a will.

[*Dies.*]

56    **Brutus . . . himself:** only Brutus conquered himself.

60    **entertain them:** take them into my service.

62    **prefer:** recommend.

67    **latest:** last.

71–72    **He, only . . . them:** He joined them only with honorable intentions for the public good.

73–75    **His life . . . man:** The Elizabethans believed that four elements (earth, water, air, and fire) in the body determined a person's temperament. Antony says that in Brutus the elements were perfectly balanced.

73    **gentle:** noble.

76    **use:** treat.

79    **ordered honorably:** with all due honor.

81    **part:** divide.

*[Alarm. Retreat. Enter* ANTONY, OCTAVIUS, MESSALA, LUCILIUS, *and the* ARMY.]

**OCTAVIUS.**    What man is that?

**MESSALA.**    My master's man. Strato, where is thy master?

**STRATO.**    Free from the bondage you are in, Messala;
55    The conquerors can but make a fire of him;
For Brutus only overcame himself,°
And no man else hath honor by his death.

**LUCILIUS.**    So Brutus should be found. I thank thee, Brutus,
That thou hast prov'd Lucilius' saying true.

60    **OCTAVIUS.**    All that serv'd Brutus, I will entertain them.°
Fellow, wilt thou bestow thy time with me?

**STRATO.**    Ay, if Messala will prefer° me to you.

**OCTAVIUS.**    Do so, good Messala.

**MESSALA.**    How died my master, Strato?

65    **STRATO.**    I held the sword, and he did run on it.

**MESSALA.**    Octavius, then take him to follow thee,
That did the latest° service to my master.

**ANTONY.**    This was the noblest Roman of them all;
All the conspirators, save only he,
70    Did that they did in envy of great Caesar;
He, only in a general honest thought
And common good to all, made one of them.°
His life was gentle,° and the elements
So mix'd in him that Nature might stand up
75    And say to all the world, "This was a man!"°

**OCTAVIUS.**    According to his virtue let us use° him,
With all respect and rites of burial.
Within my tent his bones tonight shall lie,
Most like a soldier, ordered honorably.°
80    So call the field to rest, and let's away,
To part° the glories of this happy day.

*[All exit.]*

# Related Readings

**Plutarch**
translated by
Rex Warner

# Caesar

from
# Fall of the Roman Republic

*In Julius Caesar, Shakespeare uses drama to show the effect of power and prestige on individuals and nations. Writing long before Shakespeare's time, Plutarch examines the life of Caesar from the point of view of a biographer, historian, and philosopher.*

CAESAR was born to do great things and to seek constantly for distinction. His many successes, so far from encouraging him to rest and to enjoy the fruits of all his labours, only served to kindle in him fresh confidence for the future, filling his mind with projects of still greater actions and with a passion for new glory, as though he had run through his stock of the old. His feelings can best be described by saying that he was competing with himself, as though he were someone else, and was struggling to make the future excel the past.

Yet this gave offence to those who looked at Caesar with envious eyes and resented his power. Certainly Cicero,[1] the orator, when someone remarked that the constellation Lyra would rise next day, remarked: 'No doubt. It had been ordered to do so'—implying that even the rising of the stars was something that people had to accept under compulsion.

But what made Caesar most openly and mortally hated was his passion to be made King. It was this which made the common people hate him for the first time, and it served as a most useful pretext for those others who had long hated him but had up to now disguised their feelings. Yet those who

---

1. Marcus Tullius Cicero tried in vain to uphold traditional republican principles.

were trying to get this honour conferred on Caesar actually spread the story among the people that it was foretold in the Sibylline books that Parthia could only be conquered by the Romans if the Roman army was led by a king, and as Caesar was coming down from Alba to Rome they ventured to salute him as 'King,' which caused a disturbance among the people. Caesar, upset by this himself, said that his name was not King but Caesar.[2] These words were received in total silence, and he went on his way looking far from pleased. Then there was an occasion when a number of extravagant honours had been voted for him in the senate, and Caesar happened to be sitting above the rostra. Here he was approached by the consuls and the praetors with the whole senate following behind; but instead of rising to receive them, he behaved to them as though they were merely private individuals and, after receiving their message, told them that his honours ought to be cut down rather than increased. This conduct of his offended not only the senate but the people as well, who felt that his treatment of the senators was an insult to the whole state. There was a general air of the deepest dejection and everyone who was in a position to do so went away at once. Caesar himself realized what he had done and immediately turned to go home. He drew back his toga and, uncovering his throat, cried out in a loud voice to his friends that he was ready to receive the blow from anyone who liked to give it to him. Later, however, he excused his behaviour on account of his illness, saying that those who suffer from it are apt to lose control of their senses if they address a large crowd while standing; in these circumstances they are very subject to fits of giddiness and may fall into convulsions and insensibility. This excuse, however, was not true. Caesar himself was perfectly willing to rise to receive the senate; but, so they say, one of his friends, or rather his flatterers, Cornelius Balbus, restrained him from doing so. 'Remember,' he said, 'that you are Caesar. You are their superior and ought to let them treat you as such.'

Another thing which caused offence was his insulting treatment of the tribunes.[3] The feast of the Lupercalia[4] was being celebrated and at this time

---

2. When people hailed Caesar as king, they used the title *Rex,* which means "king" in Latin but was also the name of an ancient Roman family, as was *Caesar*. According to some sources, Caesar responded by saying, "I am Caesar and no Rex!"—thus asserting his membership in the Caesar family, not the Rex family. He was also, of course, rejecting the kingly title, which had been held in contempt by Romans for generations, insisting that his own name had greater dignity.

3. officials of the Roman republic responsible for protecting common citizens against violation of their rights by magistrates of the patrician class (members of the original citizen families of ancient Rome)

4. ancient Roman festival celebrated February 15 to ensure fertility for people, fields, and livestock

many of the magistrates and many young men of noble families run through the city. Caesar, sitting on a golden throne above the rostra and wearing a triumphal robe, was watching this ceremony; and Antony,[5] who was consul at the time, was one of those taking part in the sacred running. When he came running into the forum, the crowd made way for him. He was carrying a diadem with a wreath of laurel tied round it, and he held this out to Caesar. His action was followed by some applause, but it was not much and it was not spontaneous. But when Caesar pushed the diadem away from him, there was a general shout of applause. Antony then offered him the diadem for the second time, and again only a few applauded, though, when Caesar again rejected it, there was applause from everyone. Caesar, finding that the experiment had proved a failure,[6] rose from his seat and ordered the wreath to be carried to the Capitol. It was then discovered that his statues had been decorated with royal diadems, and two of the tribunes, Flavius and Marullus, went round the statues and tore down the decorations. They then found out who had been the first to salute Caesar as King, and led them off to prison. The people followed the tribunes and were loud in their applause, calling them Brutuses—because it was Brutus[7] who first put an end to the line of Kings in Rome and gave to the senate and the people the power that had previously been in the hands of one man. This made Caesar angry. He deprived Marullus and Flavius of their tribuneship and in speaking against them he insulted the people at the same time, frequently referring to them as Brutes and Cymaeans.

It was in these circumstances that people began to turn their thoughts towards Marcus Brutus. He was thought to be, on his father's side, a descendant of the Brutus who had abolished the monarchy; on his mother's side he came from another famous family, the Servilii; and he was a son-in-law and a nephew of Cato.[8] But his own zeal for destroying the new monarchy was

---

5. Marcus Antonius (Mark Antony), friend and relative of Caesar, had held successively higher government offices, culminating in the consulship with Caesar in 44 B.C.

6. Plutarch implies that the coronation attempt was staged, perhaps by Caesar himself, to gauge the popularity of his pursuit of kingship. Caesar did take the opportunity to publicly end speculation that he sought to be made king, refusing it while saying that "Jupiter . . . alone is king of the Romans" and then publishing this official notice: "To Gaius Caesar, perpetual dictator, Marcus Antonius, the consul, by command of the people offered the kingship; Caesar was unwilling." Caesar's enemies claimed that he had refused the kingship only because the people had not applauded the offer.

7. Decimus Junius Brutus (6th century B.C.), one of Rome's first two consuls whom legend credited with helping drive out the last of the oppressive Tarquin kings of Rome

8. Marcus Porcius Cato (95–46 B.C.), leader of the political faction that defended the traditional rule of the nobility against Caesar's efforts to reform the Roman state; a supporter of Pompey against Caesar in the civil war

blunted by the honours and favours which he had received from Caesar. It was not only that at Pharsalus after Pompey's flight his own life had been spared and the lives of many of his friends at his request; he was also a person in whom Caesar had particular trust. He had been given the most important of the praetorships for this very year[9] and was to be consul three years later. For this post he had been preferred to Cassius,[10] who had been the rival candidate. Caesar, indeed, is said to have admitted that Cassius had the better claims of the two for the office. 'But,' he added, 'I cannot pass over Brutus.' And once, when the conspiracy was already formed and some people were actually accusing Brutus to Caesar of being involved in it, Caesar laid his hand on his body and said to the accusers: 'Brutus will wait for this skin of mine'—implying that Brutus certainly had the qualities which would entitle him to power, but that he would not, for the sake of power, behave basely and ungratefully.

However, those who were eager for the change and who looked to Brutus as the only, or at least the most likely, man to bring it about, used, without venturing to approach him personally, to come by night and leave papers all over the platform and the chair where he sat to do his work as praetor. Most of the messages were of this kind: 'You are asleep, Brutus' or 'You are no real Brutus.' And when Cassius observed that they were having at least something of an effect on Brutus's personal pride, he redoubled his own efforts to incite him further. Cassius, as I have mentioned in my *Life of Brutus*, had reasons of his own for hating Caesar; moreover, Caesar was suspicious of him, and once said to his friends: 'What do you think Cassius is aiming at? Personally I am not too fond of him; he is much too pale.' And on another occasion it is said that, when Antony and Dolabella were accused to him of plotting a revolution, Caesar said: 'I'm not much afraid of these fat, long-haired people. It's the other type I'm more frightened of, the pale thin ones'—by which he meant Brutus and Cassius.

Fate, however, seems to be not so much unexpected as unavoidable. Certainly, before this event, they say that strange signs were shown and strange apparitions were seen. As for the lights in the sky, the crashing sounds heard in all sorts of directions by night, the solitary specimens of birds coming down into the forum, all these, perhaps, are scarcely worth mentioning in connection with so great an event as this. But the philosopher

---

9. This would have been the urban praetorship of 44 B.C. Urban praetors dealt with legal cases involving the citizens of Rome; foreign praetors dealt with cases involving foreigners.

10. Gaius Cassius Longinus, general who had sided with Pompey against Caesar but had been pardoned by Caesar and advanced by him to a praetorship

Strabo says that a great crowd of men all on fire were seen making a charge; also that from the hand of a soldier's slave a great flame sprang out so that the hand seemed to the spectators to be burning away; but when the flame died out, the man was uninjured. He also says that when Caesar himself was making a sacrifice, the heart of the animal being sacrificed was missing—a very bad omen indeed, since in the ordinary course of nature no animal can exist without a heart. There is plenty of authority too for the following story: a soothsayer warned Caesar to be on his guard against a great danger on the day of the month of March which the Romans call the Ides; and when this day had come, Caesar, on his way to the senate-house, met the soothsayer and greeted him jestingly with the words: 'Well, the Ides of March have come,' to which the soothsayer replied in a soft voice: 'Yes, but they have not yet gone.' And on the previous day Marcus Lepidus was entertaining Caesar at supper and Caesar, according to his usual practice, happened to be signing letters as he reclined at table. Meanwhile the conversation turned to the question of what sort of death was the best, and, before anyone else could express a view on the subject, Caesar cried out: 'The kind that comes unexpectedly.' After this, when he was sleeping as usual by the side of his wife, all the doors and windows of the bedroom flew open at once; Caesar, startled by the noise and by the light of the moon shining down on him, noticed that Calpurnia[11] was fast asleep, but she was saying something in her sleep which he could not make out and was groaning in an inarticulate way. In fact she was dreaming at that time that she was holding his murdered body in her arms and was weeping over it. Though some say that it was a different dream which she had. They say that she dreamed that she saw the gable-ornament of the house torn down and for this reason fancied that she was weeping and lamenting. (This ornament, according to Livy, was put up by decree of the senate as a mark of honour and distinction.) In any case, when it was day, she implored Caesar, if it was possible, not to go out and begged him to postpone the meeting of the senate; or if, she said, he had no confidence in her dreams, then he ought to inquire about the future by sacrifices and other methods of divination. Caesar himself, it seems, was affected and by no means easy in his mind; for he had never before noticed any womanish superstition in Calpurnia and now he could see that she was in very great distress. And when the prophets, after making many sacrifices, told him that the omens were unfavourable, he decided to send for Antony and to dismiss the senate.

At this point Decimus Brutus, surnamed Albinus, intervened. Caesar had such confidence in him that he had made him the second heir in his

---

11. (Calpurnia) Roman noblewoman who had married Caesar in 59 B.C.

will, yet he was in the conspiracy with the other Brutus and Cassius. Now, fearing that if Caesar escaped this day the whole plot would come to light, he spoke derisively of the prophets and told Caesar that he ought not to give the senate such a good opportunity for thinking that they were being treated discourteously; they had met, he said, on Caesar's instructions, and they were ready to vote unanimously that Caesar should be declared King of all the provinces outside Italy with the right of wearing a diadem in any other place except Italy, whether on sea or land; but if, when they were already in session, someone were to come and tell them that they must go away for the time being and come back again when Calpurnia had better dreams, it would be easy to imagine what Caesar's enemies would have to say themselves and what sort of a reception they would give to Caesar's friends when they tried to prove that Caesar was not a slave-master or a tyrant. If, however, he had really made up his mind to treat this day as inauspicious, then, Decimus Brutus said, it would be better for him to go himself to the senate, speak personally to the senators, and adjourn the meeting.

While he was speaking, Brutus took Caesar by the hand and began to lead him towards the door. And before he had gone far from the door a slave belonging to someone else tried to approach him, but being unable to get near him because of the crowds who pressed round him, forced his way into the house and put himself into the hands of Calpurnia, asking her to keep him safe until Caesar came back, since he had some very important information to give him.

Then there was Artemidorus, a Cnidian by birth, and a teacher of Greek philosophy who, for that reason, had become acquainted with Brutus and his friends. He had thus acquired a very full knowledge of the conspiracy and he came to Caesar with a small document in which he had written down the information which he intended to reveal to him. But when he saw that Caesar took each document that was given to him and then handed it to one of his attendants, he came close up to him and said: 'Read this one, Caesar, and read it quickly and by yourself. I assure you that it is important and that it concerns you personally.' Caesar then took the document and was several times on the point of reading it, but was prevented from doing so by the numbers of people who came to speak to him. It was the only document which he did keep with him and he was still holding it in his hand when he went on into the senate. (According to some accounts, it was another person who gave him this document, and Artemidorus was kept back by the crowd all along the route and failed to get near Caesar at all.)

It may be said that all these things could have happened as it were by chance. But the place where the senate was meeting that day and which was to be the scene of the final struggle and of the assassination made it perfectly clear that some heavenly power was at work, guiding the action and directing that it should take place just here. For here stood a statue of Pompey, and the building had been erected and dedicated by Pompey as one of the extra amenities attached to his theatre. Indeed it is said that, just before the attack was made on him, Caesar turned his eyes towards the statue of Pompey and silently prayed for its goodwill. This was in spite of the fact that Caesar was a follower of the doctrines of Epicurus;[12] yet the moment of crisis, so it would seem, and the very imminence of the dreadful deed made him forget his former rationalistic views and filled him with an emotion that was intuitive or divinely inspired.

Now Antony, who was a true friend of Caesar's and also a strong man physically, was detained outside the senate house by Brutus Albinus, who deliberately engaged him in a long conversation. Caesar himself went in and the senate rose in his honour. Some of Brutus's party took their places behind his chair and others went to meet him as though they wished to support the petition being made by Tillius Cimber on behalf of his brother who was in exile. So, all joining in with him in his entreaties, they accompanied Caesar to his chair. Caesar took his seat and continued to reject their request; as they pressed him more and more urgently, he began to grow angry with them. Tillius then took hold of his toga with both hands and pulled it down from his neck. This was the signal for the attack. The first blow was struck by Casca, who wounded Caesar in the neck with his dagger. The wound was not mortal and not even a deep one, coming as it did from a man who was no doubt much disturbed in mind at the beginning of such a daring venture. Caesar, therefore, was able to turn round and grasp the knife and hold on to it. At almost the same moment the striker of the blow and he who was struck cried out together—Caesar, in Latin, 'Casca, you villain, what are you doing?' while Casca called to his brother in Greek: 'Help, brother.'

So it began, and those who were not in the conspiracy were so horrorstruck and amazed at what was being done that they were afraid to run away and afraid to come to Caesar's help; they were too afraid even to utter a word. But those who had come prepared for the murder all bared their daggers and hemmed Caesar in on every side. Whichever way he turned he met the blows of daggers and saw the cold steel aimed at his face and at his eyes. So he was driven this way and that, and like a wild beast in the toils, had to suffer from the hands of each one of them; for it had been agreed that they must

---

12. Greek philosopher (341–270 B.C.), popular in first-century B.C. Rome, who argued that death is nothing to fear: since, as he believed, the soul dissolves when the body does, there is no afterlife to feel anxious about

all take part in this sacrifice and all flesh themselves with his blood. Because of this compact Brutus also gave him one wound in the groin. Some say that Caesar fought back against all the rest, darting this way and that to avoid the blows and crying out for help, but when he saw that Brutus had drawn his dagger, he covered his head with his toga and sank down to the ground. Either by chance or because he was pushed there by his murderers, he fell down against the pedestal on which the statue of Pompey stood, and the pedestal was drenched with his blood, so that one might have thought that Pompey himself was presiding over this act of vengeance against his enemy, who lay there at his feet struggling convulsively under so many wounds. He is said to have received twenty-three wounds. And many of his assailants were wounded by each other, as they tried to plant all those blows in one body.

So Caesar was done to death, and when it was over, Brutus stepped forward with the intention of making a speech to explain what had been done. The senators, however, would not wait to hear him. They rushed out through the doors of the building and fled to their homes, thus producing a state of confusion, terror, and bewilderment, amongst the people. Some bolted their doors; others left their counters and shops and could be observed either running to see the place where Caesar had been killed or, once they had seen it, running back again. Antony and Lepidus, who were Caesar's chief friends, stole away and hid in houses belonging to other people. Brutus and his party, on the other hand, just as they were, still hot and eager from the murder, marched all together in one body from the senate house to the Capitol, holding up their naked daggers in front them and, far from giving the impression that they wanted to escape, looking glad and confident. They called out to the people that liberty had been restored, and they invited the more distinguished persons whom they met to join in with them. Some of these did join in the procession and go up with them to the Capitol, pretending that they had taken part in the deed and thus claiming their share in the glory of it. Among these were Gaius Octavius and Lentulus Spinther who suffered later for their imposture. They were put to death by Antony and young Caesar,[13] and did not even have the satisfaction of enjoying the fame which caused their death, since no one believed that they had taken part in the action. Even those who inflicted the death

---

13. Born Gaius Octavius (Octavian), the teenage Octavian's talents won him such high favor with his great-uncle Caesar that Caesar made him his chief heir and adopted son in his will (45 B.C.). After Caesar died and his will became known, Octavian took the name Gaius Julius Caesar and championed his great-uncle's cause. He joined Mark Antony in defeating Brutus and Cassius at Philippi and eventually became the first Roman emperor (27 B.C.), receiving the title Augustus ("exalted, sacred"). Though he came to hold absolute power, he carefully maintained the trappings of the republic.

penalty on them were punishing them not for what they did but for what they would have liked to have done.

Next day Brutus and his party came down from the Capitol and Brutus made a speech. The people listened to what he said without expressing either pleasure or resentment at what had been done. Their complete silence indicated that they both pitied Caesar and respected Brutus. The senate passed a decree of amnesty and tried to reconcile all parties. It was voted that Caesar should be worshipped as a god and that there should be no alteration made, however small, in any of the measures passed by him while he was in power. On the other hand, provinces and appropriate honours were given to Brutus and his friends. Everyone thought, therefore, that things were not only settled but settled in the best possible way.

But when Caesar's will was opened and it was discovered that he had left a considerable legacy to each Roman citizen, and when the people saw his body, all disfigured with its wounds, being carried through the forum, they broke through all bounds of discipline and order. They made a great pile of benches, railings, and tables from the forum and, placing the body upon this, burned it there. Then, carrying blazing brands, they ran to set fire to the houses of the murderers, while others went up and down through the city trying to find the men themselves to tear them to pieces. They, however, were well barricaded and not one of them came in the way of the mob. But there was a man called Cinna, one of Caesar's friends, who, they say, happened to have had a strange dream during the previous night. He dreamed that Caesar invited him to supper and he declined the invitation; Caesar then led him along by the hand, though he did not want to go and was pulling in the opposite direction. Now when Cinna heard that they were burning Caesar's body in the forum he got up and went there out of respect for his memory, though he felt a certain amount of misgiving as a result of his dream and was also suffering from a fever. One of the crowd who saw him there asked who he was and, when he had learned the name, told it to another. So the name was passed on and it was quickly accepted by everyone that here was one of the men who had murdered Caesar; since among the conspirators there was in fact a man with this same name of Cinna.[14] The crowd, thinking that this was he, rushed on him and tore him limb from limb on the spot. It was this more than anything else which frightened Brutus and Cassius, and within a few days they withdrew from the city. What they did and what happened to them before they died has been related in my *Life of Brutus*.

---

14. Gaius Helvius Cinna—tribune loyal to Caesar, poet and friend of the great lyric poet Catullus—was murdered by the mob when mistaken for the praetor Lucius Cornelius Cinna.

Caesar was fifty-six years old when he died. He had survived Pompey by not much more than four years. As for the supreme power which he had pursued during the whole course of his life throughout such dangers and which at last and with such difficulty he had achieved, the only fruit he reaped from it was an empty name and a glory which made him envied by his fellow-citizens. But that great divine power or genius, which had watched over him and helped him in his life, even after his death remained active as an avenger of his murder, pursuing and tracking down the murderers over every land and sea until not one of them was left and visiting with retribution all, without exception, who were in any way concerned either with the death itself or with the planning of it.

So far as human coincidences are concerned, the most remarkable was that which concerned Cassius. After his defeat at Philippi he killed himself with the very same dagger which he had used against Caesar. And of supernatural events there was, first, the great comet, which shone very brightly for seven nights after Caesar's murder and then disappeared; and also the dimming of the sun. For the whole of that year the sun's orb rose dull and pale; the heat which came down from it was feeble and ineffective, so that the atmosphere, with insufficient warmth to penetrate it, lay dark and heavy on the earth and fruits and vegetables never properly ripened, withering away and falling off before they were mature because of the coldness of the air.

But, more than anything else, the phantom which appeared to Brutus made it clear that the murder of Caesar was not pleasing to the gods. The story is as follows: Brutus was about to take his army across from Abydos to the mainland on the other side of the straits,[15] and one night was lying down, as usual, in his tent, not asleep, but thinking about the future. (It is said that of all military commanders Brutus was the one who needed least sleep, and had the greatest natural capacity for staying awake for long hours on end.) He fancied that he heard a noise at the entrance to the tent and, looking towards the light of the lamp which was almost out, he saw a terrible figure, like a man, though unnaturally large and with a very severe expression. He was frightened at first, but, finding that this apparition just stood silently by his bed without doing or saying anything, he said: 'Who are you?' Then the phantom replied: 'Brutus, I am your evil genius. You shall see me at Philippi.' On this occasion Brutus answered courageously: 'Then I shall see you,' and the supernatural visitor at once went away. Time passed and he drew up his army against Antony and Caesar near Philippi. In the

---

15. from the town of Abydos in northwestern Asia Minor to the mainland of southeastern Europe on the other side of a narrow body of water called the Hellespont, or Dardanelles, which connects the present-day Sea of Marmara with the Aegean Sea.

first battle he conquered the enemy divisions that were opposed to him, and, after routing them, broke through and sacked Caesar's camp. But in the night before the second battle the same phantom visited him again. It spoke no word, but Brutus realized that his fate was upon him and exposed himself to every danger in the battle. He did not die, however, in the fighting. It was after his troops had been routed that he retired to a steep rocky place, put his naked sword to his breast and with the help of a friend, so they say, who assisted him in driving the blow home, killed himself.

| Mark Twain | # The Killing of Julius Caesar "Localized" |

*With his typical humorous style, Mark Twain views the death of Julius Caesar through the eyes of a newspaper reporter happily covering a good story about a "bloody and mysterious murder."*

BEING THE ONLY TRUE AND RELIABLE ACCOUNT EVER PUBLISHED; TAKEN FROM THE ROMAN "DAILY EVENING FASCES," OF THE DATE OF THAT TREMENDOUS OCCURRENCE.

NOTHING in the world affords a newspaper reporter so much satisfaction as gathering up the details of a bloody and mysterious murder, and writing them up with aggravated circumstantiality. He takes a living delight in this labor of love—for such it is to him—especially if he knows that all the other papers have gone to press, and his will be the only one that will contain the dreadful intelligence. A feeling of regret has often come over me that I was not reporting in Rome when Caesar was killed—reporting on an evening paper, and the only one in the city, and getting at least twelve hours ahead of the morning paper boys with this most magnificent "item" that ever fell to the lot of the craft. Other events have happened as startling as this, but none that possessed so peculiarly all the characteristics of the favorite "item" of the present day, magnified into grandeur and sublimity by the high rank, fame, and social and political standing of the actors in it. In imagination I have seen myself skirmishing around old Rome, button-holing soldiers,

**168**    RELATED READINGS

senators, and citizens by turns, and transferring "all the particulars" from them to my notebook; and, better still, arriving at the base of Pompey's statue in time to say persuasively to the dying Caesar, "Oh! come now, you ain't so far gone, you know, but what you could stir yourself up a little and tell a fellow just how this thing happened, if you was a mind to, couldn't you?—now do!" and get the "straight of it" from his own lips, and be envied by the morning paper hounds!

Ah! if I had lived in those days, I would have written up that item gloatingly, and spiced it with a little moralizing here and plenty of blood there; and some dark, shuddering mystery; and praise and pity for some, and misrepresentation and abuse for others, (who did not patronize the paper,) and gory gashes, and notes of warning as to the tendency of the times, and extravagant descriptions of the excitement in the Senate house and the street, and all that sort of thing.

However, as I was not permitted to report Caesar's assassination in the regular way, it has at least afforded me rare satisfaction to translate the following able account of it from the original Latin of the *Roman Daily Evening Fasces* of that date—second edition.

"Our usually quiet city of Rome was thrown into a state of wild excitement yesterday by the occurrence of one of those bloody affrays which sicken the heart and fill the soul with fear, while they inspire all thinking men with forebodings for the future of a city where human life is held so cheaply, and the gravest laws are so openly set at defiance. As the result of that affray, it is our painful duty, as public journalists, to record the death of one or our most esteemed citizens—a man whose name is known wherever this paper circulates, and whose fame it has been our pleasure and our privilege to extend, and also to protect from the tongue of slander and falsehood, to the best of our poor ability. We refer to Mr. J. Caesar, the Emperor-elect.

"The facts of the case, as nearly as our reporter could determine them from the conflicting statements of eye-witnesses, were about as follows: The affair was an election row, of course. Nine tenths of the ghastly butcheries that disgrace the city nowadays grow out of the bickerings and jealousies and animosities engendered by these accursed elections. Rome would be the gainer by it if her very constables were elected to serve a century; for in our experience we have never even been able to choose a dog-pelter without celebrating the event with a dozen knock-downs and a general cramming of the station-house with drunken vagabonds over night. It is said that when the immense majority for Caesar at the polls in the market was declared the other day, and the crown was offered to that gentleman, even his amazing unselfishness in refusing it three times was not sufficient to save him from the whispered insults of such men as Casca, of the Tenth Ward, and other hirelings of the disappointed candidate, hailing mostly from the Eleventh and Thirteenth and other outside districts, who were overheard speaking ironically and contemptuously of Mr. Caesar's conduct upon that occasion.

"We are further informed that there are many among us who think they are justified in believing that the assassination of Julius Caesar was a put up thing—a cut-and-dried arrangement, hatched by Marcus Brutus and a lot of his hired roughs, and carried out only too faithfully according to the programme. Whether there be good grounds for this suspicion or not, we leave to the people to judge for themselves, only asking that they will read the following account of the sad occurrence carefully and dispassionately before they render that judgment.

"The Senate was already in session, and Caesar was coming down the street toward the capitol, conversing with some personal friends, and followed, as usual, by a large number of citizens. Just as he was passing in front of Demosthenes & Thucydides's drug-store, he was observing casually to a gentleman, who, our informant thinks, is a fortune-teller, that the Ides of March were come. The reply was, 'Yes, they are come, but not gone yet.' At this moment Artemidorus stepped up and passed the time of day, and asked Caesar to read a schedule or a tract, or something of the kind, which he had brought for his perusal. Mr. Decius Brutus also said something about an 'humble suit' which *he* wanted read. Artemidorus begged that attention might be paid to his first, because it was of personal consequence to Caesar. The latter replied that what concerned himself should be read last, or words to that effect. Artemidorus begged and beseeched him to read the paper instantly. However, Caesar shook him off, and refused to read any petition in the street. He then entered the capitol, and the crowd followed him.

"About this time the following conversation was overheard, and we consider that, taken in connection with the events which succeeded it, it bears an appalling significance: Mr. Papilius Lena remarked to George W. Cassius, (commonly known as the 'Nobby Boy of the Third Ward,') a bruiser in the pay of the Opposition, that he hoped his enterprise to-day might thrive; and when Cassius asked, 'What enterprise?' he only closed his left eye temporarily and said with simulated indifference, 'Fare you well,' and sauntered toward Caesar. Marcus Brutus, who is suspected of being the ringleader of the band that killed Caesar, asked what it was that Lena had said. Cassius told him, and added in a low tone, '*I fear our purpose is discovered.*'

"Brutus told his wretched accomplice to keep an eye on Lena, and a moment after Cassius urged that lean and hungry vagrant, Casca, whose reputation here is none of the best, to be sudden, for he *feared prevention*. He then turned to Brutus, apparently much excited, and asked what should be done, and swore that either he or Caesar *should never turn back*—he would kill himself first. At this time Caesar was talking to some of the back-country members about the approaching fall elections, and paying little attention to what was going on around him. Billy Trebonius got into conversation with the people's friend and Caesar's—Mark Antony—and under some pretense or other got him away, and Brutus, Decius Casca, Cinna, Metellus Cimber, and others of the gang of infamous desperadoes that infest Rome at present, closed around the doomed Caesar. Then Metellus Cimber knelt down and begged that his brother might be recalled from banishment, but Caesar rebuked him for his fawning, sneaking conduct, and refused to grant his petition. Immediately, at Cimber's request, first Brutus and then Cassius begged for the return of the banished Publius; but Caesar still refused. He said he could not be moved; that he was as fixed as the North Star, and proceeded to speak in the most complimentary terms of the firmness of that star, and its steady character. Then he said he was like it, and he believed he was the only man in the country that was; therefore, since he was 'constant' that Cimber should be banished, he was also 'constant' that he should stay banished, and he'd be d—d if he didn't keep him so!

"Instantly seizing upon this shallow pretext for a fight, Casca sprang at Caesar and struck him with a dirk, Caesar grabbing him by the arm with his right hand, and launching a blow straight from the shoulder with his left, that sent the reptile bleeding to the earth. He then backed up against Pompey's statue, and squared himself to receive his assailants. Cassius and Cimber and Cinna rushed upon him with their daggers drawn, and the former succeeded in inflicting a wound upon his body; but before he could strike again, and before either of the others could strike at all, Caesar stretched the three miscreants at his feet with as many blows of his powerful fist. By this time the Senate was in an indescribable uproar; the throng of citizens in the lobbies had blockaded the doors in their frantic efforts to escape from the building, the sergeant-at-arms and his assistants were struggling with the assassins, venerable senators had cast aside their encumbering robes, and were leaping over benches and flying down the aisles in wild confusion toward the shelter of the committee-rooms, and a thousand voices were shouting, 'Po-lice! Po-lice!' in discordant tones that rose above the frightful din like shrieking winds above the roaring of a tempest. And amid it all, great Caesar stood with his back against the statue, like a lion at bay, and fought his assailants weaponless and hand to hand, with the defiant bearing and unwavering courage which he had shown before on many a bloody field. Billy Trebonius and Caius Legarius struck him with their daggers and fell, as their brother-conspirators before them had fallen. But at last, when Caesar saw his old friend Brutus step forward, armed with a murderous knife, it is said he seemed utterly overpowered with grief and amazement, and dropping his invincible left arm by his side, he hid his face in the folds of his mantle and received the treacherous blow without an effort to stay the hand that gave it. He only said, '*Et tu, Brute?*' and fell lifeless on the marble pavement.

"We learn that the coat deceased had on when he was killed was the same he wore in his tent on the afternoon of the day he overcame the Nervii, and that when it was removed from the corpse it was found to be cut and gashed in no less than seven different places. There was nothing in the pockets. It will be exhibited at the coroner's inquest, and will be damning proof of the fact of the killing. These latter facts may be relied on, as we get them from Mark Antony, whose position enables him to learn every item of news connected with the one subject of absorbing interest of to-day.

"LATER.—While the coroner was summoning a jury, Mark Antony and other friends of the late Caesar got hold of the body, and lugged it off to the Forum, and at last accounts Antony and Brutus were making speeches over it and raising such a row among the people that, as we go to press, the chief of police is satisfied there is going to be a riot, and is taking measures accordingly."

Robert F.
Kennedy

# On the Death of Martin Luther King

*On April 4, 1968, Robert Kennedy was flying to
Indianapolis to appear at a campaign rally in his bid for the
Democratic nomination for President. On his way to the
rally, Kennedy heard of the assassination of Dr. Martin
Luther King, Jr. Although he was advised to cancel his
appearance, Kennedy appeared at the rally, stepped onto
the platform, and shared with his audience the tragic news.*

LADIES AND GENTLEMEN—I'm only going to talk to you just for a
minute or so this evening. Because . . .

I have some very sad news for all of you, and I think sad news for all of our
fellow citizens, and people who love peace all over the world, and that is
that Martin Luther King was shot and was killed tonight in Memphis,
Tennessee.

Martin Luther King dedicated his life to love and to justice between fellow
human beings. He died in the cause of that effort. In this difficult day, in
this difficult time for the United States, it's perhaps well to ask what kind of
a nation we are and what direction we want to move in.

For those of you who are black—considering the evidence evidently is that
there were white people who were responsible—you can be filled with bit-
terness, and with hatred, and a desire for revenge.

We can move in that direction as a country, in greater polarization—black
people amongst blacks, and white amongst whites, filled with hatred toward
one another. Or we can make an effort, as Martin Luther King did, to understand and to comprehend, and replace that violence, that stain of bloodshed

that has spread across our land, with an effort to understand, compassion and love.

For those of you who are black and are tempted to be filled with hatred and mistrust of the injustice of such an act, against all white people, I would only say that I can also feel in my own heart the same kind of feeling. I had a member of my family killed, but he was killed by a white man.

But we have to make an effort in the United States, we have to make an effort to understand, to get beyond these rather difficult times.

My favorite poet was Aeschylus. He once wrote: "Even in our sleep, pain which cannot forget falls drop by drop upon the heart, until, in our own despair, against our will, comes wisdom through the awful grace of God."

What we need in the United States is not division; what we need in the United States is not hatred; what we need in the United States is not violence and lawlessness, but is love and wisdom, and compassion toward one another, and a feeling of justice toward those who still suffer within our country, whether they be white or whether they be black.

*(Interrupted by applause)*

So I ask you tonight to return home, to say a prayer for the family of Martin Luther King, yeah that's true, but more importantly to say a prayer for our own country, which all of us love—a prayer for understanding and that compassion of which I spoke. We can do well in this country. We will have difficult times. We've had difficult times in the past. And we will have difficult times in the future. It is not the end of violence; it is not the end of lawlessness; and it's not the end of disorder.

But the vast majority of white people and the vast majority of black people in this country want to live together, want to improve the quality of our life, and want justice for all human beings that abide in our land.

*(Interrupted by applause)*

Let us dedicate ourselves to what the Greeks wrote so many years ago: to tame the savageness of man and make gentle the life of this world.

Let us dedicate ourselves to that, and say a prayer for our country and for our people. Thank you very much. *(Applause)*

Robert F. Kennedy—April 4, 1968

# Chinua Achebe

# The Voter

*Certain factions among the common people and the political leaders in the time of Julius Caesar rallied to support Caesar, while others sought to bring about his downfall. In this story by Chinua Achebe, a more modern society faces decisions about how they will choose their leaders.*

R UFUS OKEKE—ROOF FOR SHORT—was a very popular man in his village. Although the villagers did not explain it in so many words Roof's popularity was a measure of their gratitude to an energetic young man who, unlike most of his fellows nowadays had not abandoned the village in order to seek work, any work, in the towns. And Roof was not a village lout either. Everyone knew how he had spent two years as a bicycle repairer's apprentice in Port Harcourt, and had given up of his own free will a bright future to return to his people and guide them in these difficult times. Not that Umuofia needed a lot of guidance. The village already belonged *en masse* to the People's Alliance Party, and its most illustrious son, Chief the Honorable Marcus Ibe, was Minister of Culture in the outgoing government (which was pretty certain to be the incoming one as well). Nobody doubted that the Honorable Minister would be elected in his constituency. Opposition to him was like the proverbial fly trying to move a dunghill. It would have been ridiculous enough without coming, as it did now, from a complete nonentity.

As was to be expected Roof was in the service of the Honorable Minister for the coming elections. He had become a real expert in election campaigning at all levels—village, local government or national. He could tell the mood and temper of the electorate at any given time. For instance he had warned the Minister months ago about the radical change that had come into the thinking of Umuofia since the last national election.

The villagers had had five years in which to see how quickly and plentifully politics brought wealth, chieftaincy titles, doctorate degrees and other honors some of which, like the last, had still to be explained satisfactorily to them; for in their naïveté they still expected a doctor to be able to heal the sick. Anyhow, these honors and benefits had come so readily to the man to whom they had given their votes free of charge five years ago that they were now ready to try it a different way.

Their point was that only the other day Marcus Ibe was a not too successful mission school teacher. Then politics had come to their village and he had wisely joined up, some said just in time to avoid imminent dismissal arising from a female teacher's pregnancy. Today he was Chief the Honorable; he had two long cars and had just built himself the biggest house anyone had seen in these parts. But let it be said that none of these successes had gone to Marcus's head as well they might. He remained devoted to his people. Whenever he could he left the good things of the capital and returned to his village which had neither running water nor electricity, although he had lately installed a private plant to supply electricity to his new house. He knew the source of his good fortune, unlike the little bird who ate and drank and went out to challenge his personal spirit. Marcus had christened his new house "Umuofia Mansions" in honor of his village, and he had slaughtered five bulls and countless goats to entertain the people on the day it was opened by the Archbishop.

Everyone was full of praise for him. One old man said: "Our son is a good man; he is not like the mortar which as soon as food comes its way turns its back on the ground." But when the feasting was over, the villagers told themselves that they had underrated the power of the ballot paper before and should not do so again. Chief the Honorable Marcus Ibe was not unprepared. He had drawn five months' salary in advance, changed a few hundred pounds into shining shillings and armed his campaign boys with eloquent little jute bags. In the day he made his speeches; at night his stalwarts conducted their whispering campaign. Roof was the most trusted of these campaigners.

"We have a Minister from our village, one of our own sons," he said to a group of elders in the house of Ogbuefi Ezenwa, a man of high traditional title. "What greater honor can a village have? Do you ever stop to ask yourselves why we should be singled out for this honor? I will tell you; it is because we are favored by the leaders of PAP. Whether or not we cast our paper for Marcus, PAP will continue to rule. Think of the pipe-borne water they have promised us . . ."

Besides Roof and his assistant there were five elders in the room. An old hurricane lamp with a cracked, sooty, glass chimney gave out yellowish light in their midst. The elders sat on very low stools. On the floor, directly in front of each of them, lay two shilling pieces. Outside beyond the fastened door, the moon kept a straight face.

"We believe every word you say to be true," said Ezenwa. "We shall, every one of us, drop his paper for Marcus. Who would leave an ozo feast and go to a poor ritual meal? Tell Marcus he has our papers, and our wives' papers too. But what we do say is that two shillings is shameful." He brought the lamp close and tilted it at the money before him as if to make sure he had not mistaken its value. "Yes, two shillings is too shameful. If Marcus were a poor man—which our ancestors forbid—I should be the first to give him my paper free, as I did before. But today Marcus is a great man and does his things like a great man. We did not ask him for money yesterday; we shall not ask him tomorrow. But today is our day; we have climbed the iroko tree today and would be foolish not to take down all the firewood we need."

Roof had to agree. He had lately been taking down a lot of firewood himself. Only yesterday he had asked Marcus for one of his many rich robes—and had got it. Last Sunday Marcus's wife (the teacher that nearly got him in trouble) had objected (like the woman she was) when Roof pulled out his fifth bottle of beer from the refrigerator; she was roundly and publicly rebuked by her husband. To cap it all Roof had won a land case re-cently because, among other things, he had been chauffeur-driven to the disputed site. So he understood the elders about the firewood.

"All right," he said in English and then reverted to Ibo. "Let us not quar-rel about small things." He stood up, adjusted his robes and plunged his hand once more into the bag. Then he bent down like a priest distributing the host and gave one shilling more to every man; only he did not put it into their palms but on the floor in front of them. The men, who had so far not deigned to touch the things, looked at the floor and shook their heads. Roof got up again and gave each man another shilling.

"I am through," he said with a defiance that was no less effective for being transparently faked. The elders too knew how far to go without losing decorum. So when Roof added: "Go cast your paper for the enemy if you like!" they quickly calmed him down with a suitable speech from each of them. By the time the last man had spoken it was possible, without great loss of dignity, to pick up the things from the floor . . .

The enemy Roof had referred to was the Progressive Organization Party (POP) which had been formed by the tribes down the coast to save them-selves, as the founders of the party proclaimed, from "total political, cul-tural, social and religious annihilation." Although it was clear the party had no chance here it had plunged, with typical foolishness, into a straight fight with PAP, providing cars and loud-speakers to a few local rascals and thugs to go around and make a lot of noise. No one knew for certain how much money POP had let loose in Umuofia but it was said to be very considerable. Their local campaigners would end up very rich, no doubt.

Up to last night everything had been "moving according to plan," as Roof would have put it. Then he had received a strange visit from the leader of the POP campaign team. Although he and Roof were well known to each other, and might even be called friends, his visit was cold and business- like. No words were wasted. He placed five pounds on the floor before Roof and said, "We want your vote." Roof got up from his chair, went to the outside door, closed it carefully and returned to his chair. The brief exercise gave him enough time to weigh the proposition. As he spoke his eyes never left the red notes on the floor. He seemed to be mesmerized by the picture of the cocoa farmer harvesting his crops.

"You know I work for Marcus," he said feebly. "It will be very bad . . ."

"Marcus will not be there when you put in your paper. We have plenty of work to do tonight; are you taking this or not?"

"It will not be heard outside this room?" asked Roof.

"We are after votes not gossip."

"All right," said Roof in English.

The man nudged his companion and he brought forward an object covered with a red cloth and proceeded to remove the cover. It was a fearsome little affair contained in a clay pot with feathers stuck into it.

"The *iyi* comes from Mbanta. You know what that means. Swear that you will vote for Maduka. If you fail to do so, this *iyi* take note."

Roof's heart nearly flew out when he saw the *iyi*; indeed he knew the fame of Mbanta in these things. But he was a man of quick decision. What could a single vote cast in secret for Maduka take away from Marcus's certain victory? Nothing.

"I will cast my paper for Maduka; if not this *iyi* take note."

"Das all," said the man as he rose with his companion who had covered up the object again and was taking it back to their car.

"You know he has no chance against Marcus," said Roof at the door.

"It is enough that he gets a few votes now; next time he will get more. People will hear that he gives out pounds, not shillings, and they will listen."

Election morning. The great day every five years when the people exercise power. Weather-beaten posters on walls of houses, tree trunks and telegraph poles. The few that were still whole called out their message to those who could read. Vote for the People's Alliance Party! Vote for the Progressive Organization Party! Vote for PAP! Vote for POP! The posters that were torn called out as much of the message as they could.

As usual Chief the Honorable Marcus Ibe was doing things in grand style. He had hired a highlife band from Umuru and stationed it at such a distance from the voting booths as just managed to be lawful. Many villagers danced to the music, their ballot papers held aloft, before proceeding to the booths. Chief the Honorable Marcus Ibe sat in the "owner's corner" of his enormous green car and smiled and nodded. One enlightened villager came up to the car, shook hands with the great man and said in advance, "Congrats!" This immediately set the pattern. Hundreds of admirers shook Marcus's hand and said "Corngrass!"

Roof and the other organizers were prancing up and down, giving last minute advice to the voters and pouring with sweat.

"Do not forget," he said again to a group of illiterate women who seemed ready to burst with enthusiasm and good humor, "our sign is the motor car . . ."

"Like the one Marcus is sitting inside."

"Thank you, mother," said Roof. "It is the same car. The box with the car shown on its body is the box for you. Don't look at the other with the man's head: it is for those whose heads are not correct."

This was greeted with loud laughter. Roof cast a quick and busy-like glance towards the Minister and received a smile of appreciation.

"Vote for the car," he shouted, all the veins in his neck standing out. "Vote for the car and you will ride in it!"

"Or if we don't, our children will," piped the same sharp, old girl.

The band struck up a new number: "Why walk when you can ride . . ."

In spite of his apparent calm and confidence Chief the Honorable Marcus was a relentless stickler for detail. He knew he would win what the newspapers called "a landslide victory" but he did not wish, even so, to throw away a single vote. So as soon as the first rush of voters was over he promptly asked his campaign boys to go one at a time and put in their ballot papers.

"Roof, you had better go first," he said.

Roof's spirits fell; but he let no one see it. All morning he had masked his deep worry with a surface exertion which was unusual even for him. Now he dashed off in his springy fashion towards the booths. A policeman at the entrance searched him for illegal ballot papers and passed him. Then the electoral officer explained to him about the two boxes. By this time the spring had gone clean out of his walk. He sidled in and was confronted by the car and the head. He brought out his ballot paper from his pocket and looked at it. How could he betray Marcus even in secret? He resolved to go back to the other man and return his five pounds . . . Five pounds! He knew at once it was impossible. He had sworn on that *iyi*. The notes were red; the cocoa farmer busy at work.

At this point he heard the muffled voice of the policeman asking the electoral officer what the man was doing inside. "Abi na pickin im de born?"

Quick as lightning a thought leapt into Roof's mind. He folded the paper, tore it in two along the crease and put one half in each box. He took the precaution of putting the first half into Maduka's box and confirming the action verbally: "I vote for Maduka."

They marked his thumb with indelible purple ink to prevent his return, and he went out of the booth as jauntily as he had gone in.

**Sandra Cisneros**

# Geraldo No Last Name

*Following the death of a great leader, such as Julius Caesar, entire nations take notice and many mourn. In this brief story, Sandra Cisneros tells about a different kind of death and mourning*

SHE MET HIM AT A DANCE. Pretty too, and young. Said he worked in a restaurant, but she can't remember which one. Geraldo. That's all. Green pants and Saturday shirt. Geraldo. That's what he told her.

And how was she to know she'd be the last one to see him alive. An accident, don't you know. Hit-and-run. Marin, she goes to all those dances. Uptown. Logan. Embassy. Palmer. Aragon. Fontana. The Manor. She likes to dance. She knows how to do cumbias and salsas and rancheras even. And he was just someone she danced with. Somebody she met that night. That's right.

That's the story. That's what she said again and again. Once to the hospital people and twice to the police. No address. No name. Nothing in his pockets. Ain't it a shame.

Only Marin can't explain why it mattered, the hours and hours, for somebody she didn't even know. The hospital emergency room. Nobody but an intern working all alone. And maybe if the surgeon would've come, maybe if he hadn't lost so much blood, if the surgeon had only come, they would know who to notify and where.

But what difference does it make? He wasn't anything to her. He wasn't her boyfriend or anything like that. Just another *brazer* who didn't speak English. Just another wetback. You know the kind. The ones who always look ashamed. And what was she doing out at three a.m. anyway? Marin who was sent home with her coat and some aspirin. How does she explain?

She met him at a dance. Geraldo in his shiny shirt and green pants. Geraldo going to a dance.

What does it matter?

They never saw the kitchenettes. They never knew about the two-room flats and sleeping rooms he rented, the weekly money orders sent home, the currency exchange. How could they?

His name was Geraldo. And his home is in another country. The ones left behind are far away, will wonder, shrug, remember. Geraldo—he went north . . . we never heard from him again.

**Garrett Hongo**

# The
# Legend

*The man in Chicago about whom Garrett Hongo writes*
*stands out in sharp contrast to the powerful Julius Caesar*
*in Shakespeare's play.*

In Chicago, it is snowing softly
and a man has just done his wash for the week.
He steps into the twilight of early evening,
carrying a wrinkled shopping bag
5    full of neatly folded clothes,
and, for a moment, enjoys
the feel of warm laundry and crinkled paper,
flannellike against his gloveless hands.
There's a Rembrandt° glow on his face,
10   a triangle of orange in the hollow of his cheek
as a last flash of sunset
blazes the storefronts and lit windows of the street.

He is Asian, Thai or Vietnamese,
and very skinny, dressed as one of the poor
15   in rumpled suit pants and a plaid mackinaw,
dingy and too large.
He negotiates the slick of ice
on the sidewalk by his car,
opens the Fairlane's back door,

---

**9. Rembrandt:** Dutch painter (1606–1669), famous for his dramatic use of
color and of light and shadow

20     leans to place the laundry in,
        and turns, for an instant,
        toward the flurry of footsteps
        and cries of pedestrians
        as a boy—that's all he was—
25     backs from the corner package store
        shooting a pistol, firing it,
        once, at the dumbfounded man
        who falls forward,
        grabbing at his chest.

30     A few sounds escape from his mouth,
        a babbling no one understands
        as people surround him
        bewildered at his speech.
        The noises he makes are nothing to them.
35     The boy has gone, lost
        in the light array of foot traffic
        dappling the snow with fresh prints.
        Tonight, I read about Descartes'
        grand courage to doubt everything
40     except his own miraculous existence
        and I feel so distinct
        from the wounded man lying on the concrete
        I am ashamed.

        Let the night sky cover him as he dies.
45     Let the weaver girl cross the bridge of heaven
        and take up his cold hands.

**IN MEMORY OF JAY KASHIWAMURA**